Happy Anniversary! #20!
Love always Ida.
xxx

WATERCRESS, WILLOW AND WINE

Enjoy! with a glass or two!

Cindy-Marie
o

A Celebration of Recipes and Wines
from English Vineyards

WATERCRESS, WILLOW AND WINE

Cindy-Marie Harvey

LOVE
WINE
FOOD
BOOKS

First published in 2022 by Love Wine Food Books

ISBN 9781913532864

Also available as an ebook
ISBN 9781913532871

Illustration by Chloe Robertson
Design by Anna Green at Siulen Design
Project management by whitefox
Printed and bound in the UK by Bell & Bain

CONTENTS

FOREWORD BY JULIA TRUSTRAM-EVE

The wine industry of Great Britain is at a pivotal moment in its history, so it couldn't be a better time to discover more about this exciting wine region. While still a relatively young member of the global wine family, this small island is already starting to conquer the hearts and minds of wine lovers, earning international awards and plaudits from wine experts around the world. Britain is neither old world nor new, but a wine region that is unique and innovative, producing a thrilling range of wines that can match the best of anywhere else in the world.

The charge is led by our classic method sparkling wines of exquisite quality that have taken the wine world by storm. Then there are the gloriously fresh, complex, aromatic and crisp still wines; fruity reds; mouthwatering light rosés and invitingly sweet wines. Then there are orange wines, wines produced in qvevri, natural wines, sparkling wines created by other methods … the list goes on, illustrating the scope and confidence this band of home-grown and international winemakers are now producing in this green and pleasant land.

The Royalty of global grape varieties, Chardonnay and Pinot Noir, have laid their roots down in our soils and are showing just what showstopping sparkling and still wines they produce. There are exciting discoveries to be made from the many other grapes that have found a great home on these shores; aromatic, fruity, fresh – we boast them all.

More and more producers are opening up their vineyards and wineries to visitors, boasting tourism experiences during which you can get to know more about our wines and the people behind them. Welcome to this exciting and wonderful world!

We travel the world to absorb the wine and gastronomic culture of different countries and regions; now we can – and should – look at what is on our own doorstep… Enjoy discovering some gems through the pages of this book to find some sublime pairings of your own!

JULIA TRUSTRAM-EVE, WINEGB

FOREWORD BY
TONY LAITHWAITE, CBE

Has anyone ever taken more people to more vineyards around the world than Cindy-Marie? I don't think so.

That lifetime of leading wine tours, meeting not only wine producers but wine lovers – and hearing them all animatedly chatting away as they do after a glass or few – must have been vital when, during the two years of inactivity we all experienced during the pandemic, she stopped rushing madly around and set about writing this scrumptious book.

I'm sure her many followers will love reading and salivating through these pages. Though I suspect they might prefer to be once again in her company as the queen of wine guides touring England, gleaning the facts.

And to those who haven't had that pleasure, I am well placed to confirm that life offers few pleasures greater than visiting vineyards, tasting wines with winemakers and afterwards tucking into glorious food with Cindy-Marie. Let this book be your key to a magical world that isn't fantasy: it actually exists.

TONY LAITHWAITE, CBE

INTRODUCTION

*Rolling hills lined with perfectly manicured vines that glisten in the summer sunshine.
Dazzling white chalk soils that urge you to reach for your sunshades.
A glass of chilled award-winning fizz in hand as you relax on a terrace enjoying the view.
Perfect food and wine pairing with seductive Pinot Noir and delicious slow-cooked lamb.*

Images that have seduced many a wine lover over the years to visit the classic vineyards of Reims and Épernay in Champagne or gastronomic Burgundy, home to world-revered wines. Or maybe the stylish sparkling wine vineyards of Franciacorta, east of Milan, or the dramatic Dolomites, the source of some of Italy's finest Pinot Noirs.

But it's time to think again. Instead, it is welcome to the exciting world of English wine. From the vineyards of the South West to the beautiful downlands of Hampshire, Sussex and Surrey, through to the Garden of England that is Kent – there has never been a better time to celebrate the wines made in England. Naturally, as wine is made to be enjoyed with food, I am incredibly pleased to showcase some of the most wonderful local produce from our land and sea, with a collection of vibrant recipes.

England's range of sparkling wines have been rightly rewarded over the last few years in blind tastings against other famous sparkling wines from around the globe. But it might come as a surprise to you that sublime still wines are also being made on our soils: crisp whites that are the perfect aperitif, delectable food-friendly rosés and even that most fickle of red grapes, Pinot Noir is happily finding its feet in a new home.

Over the next few pages, you will discover a selection of my favourite estates. It has been a heart-wrenchingly difficult decision to select a single wine to feature with its own matched recipe. So I have mentioned some of the others along the way to tempt you to explore the panoply of styles now being made in England. At the end of the book, I have listed the estates' websites and where to buy their wines.

We should also be immensely proud of the diversity of local foods made with love and care by boutique and artisanal producers in England. A number of them take inspiration from abroad, such as the fabulous range of charcuterie now made, cured and smoked in the UK, while others are re-establishing food production values sadly forgotten in the mass-production era, where flavour and quality have been compromised. It is my pleasure to suggest for each wine, as well as an actual recipe, an idea for what I call an *assemblage*. Simply source some excellent local produce that needs no more than unwrapping and arranging on an attractive platter – for those days when that is *quite* enough of a culinary effort!

English Vineyards

Vines have been grown in England since the mists of time, to use that well-known phrase. The reason for that suitably vague description is that there is a difference of opinion as to whether the Romans or the Normans were responsible for their introduction. What is certainly the case is that today there is a true renaissance of vine growing and an explosion of new plantings, resulting in over 800 domestic vineyards across England, Wales and even Scotland as of 2022 and that number is increasing rapidly.

From my home in the South Downs National Park in Hampshire, it has now become the norm to see vineyards planted as much as other crops; this part of England is, after all, so suited to grape growing. Hectarage under vine has more than doubled in just eight years and, in the past five years the amount of land under vine has increased by 70%.

The counties of South East and South West England have the lion's share of vines, with 526 vineyards. The rest of the UK has about 800 vineyards (including about 30 in Wales).

After the Second World War there were several very enthusiastic pioneers of

English wine, notable among them Major-General Sir Guy Salisbury-Jones who, in 1952, planted Hambledon Vineyard in Hampshire. However, owing to the less-than-ideal climatic conditions of the time, these early vineyards were mostly planted with Germanic grape varieties – Müller-Thurgau, Huxelrebe and Reichensteiner – which tended to be early ripening and highly acidic. Swipe forward a few decades, and we find a handful of key families who passionately believed in the future of quality English wine. These included Bob and Annie Lindo at Camel Valley in Cornwall, Mike Roberts at Ridgeview, and the Moss family, whose estate is now Nyetimber, respectively in East and West Sussex and the Ash family at Sharpham in Devon. They all in turn inspired the vast wave of winemakers and vineyard owners that have followed their ambitious lead in the past ten to twenty plus years (remember that nothing happens quickly in vineyard terms!)

One of the most important events of recent times was the spectacular 2018 vintage, which was as perfect as any winemaker could hope for – both in terms of quality and quantity. Indeed, although the level of quality was a delight to behold (and drink!), the leap in the sheer volume of ripe grapes ready to be picked presented its own challenges, with many an unexpected container being pressed into use as a vat during harvest.

Sustainability is a key area of focus for many of the English estates, which has led to the creation of a new scheme, Sustainable Wines of Great Britain (SWGB), dedicated to observing key sustainable practices throughout, such as using renewable energy to reduce the carbon footprint of every bottle produced, encouraging biodiversity, soil conservation and minimal intervention in the form of pesticides and fertilisers to ensure the rapid expansion of English vineyards does not create a negative ecological impact.

The future of English wine is blossoming on so many fronts. Despite the challenges and disruption brought about by Covid-19, exports rose by 51% in the 12 months from September 2020. Sparkling wine exports have risen by 33%, while there was a 501% growth in shipments of still wine. Still wine now represents 17% of total exports. Key market growth has come from Scandinavia, which now represents 63% of all exports. British wine is shipped to thirty export markets, but the top ten represent 92% of total shipments.

Understanding of vineyard sites is improving, as is how to cope with climatic variations. But a word of caution must be sounded, given the speed with which vineyards are being planted: can the sparkling wine market sustain such rapid growth?

Another factor we cannot ignore is climate change. Away from the so-called *glamorous* world of wine, it is easy to forget that grapes are an agriculture crop like any other, subject to disease, pests and at the mercy of the weather: rain (too little or too much at the wrong time), temperature changes and hours of sunshine. It is interesting to note that the last time in recorded history that vine growing was widespread in England coincided with a cycle of warmer climates known as the

Medieval Warm period between the tenth and thirteenth centuries. Whatever your views on the timescales of climate change, weather systems in cool-climate Britain, at the margins of where it is possible to ripen grapes, *are* changing, a factor that may have contributed to the long-term decision of several leading French champagne houses to invest in land for vineyards in southern England. One outcome of global warming is that our ripening season is now extended, which means that the grapes get longer 'hang time' on the vines, achieve better phenolic ripeness, which in turn allows more flavour to become expressed as ultimately better-balanced and complex wine in the glass. This increase in warmth is not only in the better-known vineyards of Kent, Sussex and Hampshire, but also across the UK, everywhere from Yorkshire to Wales. Indeed, there is a lot of excited chatter suggesting that Essex may well be one of the leading areas for quality grape-growing in England.

Grape Varieties

The classic trio of Champagne grapes – Chardonnay, Pinot Noir and Meunier make up over half of the vineyard plantings in the UK. This is not surprising, given that there are many vineyard plantings in the South, especially in Kent, Sussex and Hampshire, that are based on the same geology that is found in Champagne. The chalk and limestone that give Champagne its fabled *terroir*, reappears on the English side of the Channel along the South Coast, with the chalk extending inland and northwards as well. Historically wine regions located at the extreme limit of grape ripening, have long made sparkling wines to tame the searing acidity from underripe grapes. The acidity is essential for quality sparkling wines, usually tempered with *dosage* (basically a finely judged tiny amount of sweetness added to the wine) to give balance. There is a growing trend to produce non-dosage sparkling wine (where no sweetness is added at all), giving a very racy but thrilling style of wine.

But there are other varieties to look out for, including what is fast becoming viewed as the flagship variety: Bacchus. With its crisp, green apple notes it leads the rollcall of white grape varieties – it is often referred to as the Sauvignon Blanc of England, although I am not completely sure the comparison is entirely fair on either variety. It does, however, tend to work incredibly well with many of the same foods that Sauv Blanc matches, such as asparagus and goat's cheese. Pinot Blanc and Pinot Gris have likewise gained much award-winning attention and are wonderfully food friendly. The Pinot Noir vines planted originally for fizz production were given a real boost by the 2018 vintage, showing lovely notes of red fruit as well as complexity – this is one variety to watch out for in red wines. There are lots of other smaller plantings but as many more varieties are being experimented with – including the white Albariño, normally found in Galicia in northern Spain, and today planted at Ancre Hill vineyard in Monmouthshire, Wales, as well as the red Gamay Noir from the brilliant estate of Biddenden in Kent – it is a fun time to be open minded and discover the diversity of English wines.

How to Pair Food and Wine

The first thing you do on opening this book, is to pour yourself a glass of wine (English, naturally), curl up comfortably and flick through the recipes for inspiration before returning in a quieter moment to read through all the intro and other 'wordy' pages – or is that just me?

Confession Time. I loathe wine snobbery. I abhor anything that transforms such a fundamental of our lives – the pleasure of food and drink – into some sort of exclusive game of one-upmanship. But equally I cannot abide the inverted snobbery that says food and wine pairing is utter twaddle! Neither extreme helps people simply wanting to find out a little more about a vast and wide-ranging subject in order to widen their horizons without feeling intimidated.

There are also many people who like wine but do not know how to get beyond their default choice of Sauvignon Blanc or Cabernet Sauvignon. They are unlikely to buy a book solely about wine for fear of being bored by technical jargon. On the other hand, there are real food lovers for whom choosing the wine is of secondary importance. Hopefully, this book will help both parties to peer over the vineyard wall and discover something wonderful and new, without feeling uneasy!

One of the most important things to realise is that there are no wrong choices. If you like drinking a certain wine with a particular style of food and it tickles your taste buds, then that is absolutely spot on. The task of this book is to showcase some wonderful pairings that increase the enjoyment of both the wine and the food, the one complementing the other.

So why should you think about which wine to pair with your food choice? Well, there are scientific reasons why some foods sing when put together with a particular style of wine, while others will appear muted, boring or positively jar. I do not want to get too technical but here are some handy references to think about when you are experimenting with your own recipes or wine choices.

Fat – Creamy, oily or fatty foods need acid in the wine to balance their richness. Think sparkling wines balancing out the creamy element of cheese, such as triple cream brie or roast pork with crackling paired with a crisp white with a fair bite of acidity.

Acid – Wines with an acidic style will bring a zing and liveliness to your food. For foods with high acidic levels, such as warm grain salad with tomatoes and preserved lemons (and doubtless vinegar in the dressing), you need to reach for a wine that has at least a similar level of acidity.

Salt – This is a difficult one because salt is prevalent in so many recipes – just be aware as it can make a fruit-driven red taste weak and thin. One of the reasons why a classic pairing for old-school fish & chips is sparkling wine is because the wine's lack of salinity (plus the bubbles) helps balance out the salt (and fat).

Sugar – This is a fun one to play with as you can get rid of any preconceptions about sugar in wine. Even in technically dry to off dry wines, the small amount of residual sugar in the wine gives body and texture rather than actual perception of sweetness – which works so well giving many foods a breadth of flavour rather than being mono-dimensional.

We are talking starters and main courses here: savoury dishes that welcome a fuller textured wine – think Asian flavours with New Zealand Pinot Gris. For dessert wines, the wine must be sweeter than the actual dessert (although personally I think most dessert wines work better enjoyed alone, or with cheese or a dish of nuts, rather than with a sticky gaudy pud.)

Weight – It is all about balance to ensure that neither the food nor the wine loses the battle of strength. So lighter styles of wines work well with lighter foods and the inverse also applies – think of a slow-braised beef and porcini casserole with a deep warming Malbec rather than an easy-quaffing Bardolino, which would be lost in the depth of the food.

Tannins – These compounds exist in the skin, seeds and stems of grapes, and therefore they are present in all wines, though most associated with reds because of the extended skin-contact during fermentation. Tannin gives structure and texture to a wine. Think what happens when you leave a tea bag in a mug to brew: the longer it rests, the more strength and bitterness it gains. But tannin is a good thing in food pairings. The levels of tannin in many red Italian wines can make them a bit of a challenge to drink on their own but when matched with a rich meaty ragu both food and wine rack it up to the next mmmm level of enjoyment.

Key Flavours – Look for a dominant flavour in your dish/recipe and see if you can link it with its best friend. For instance, a buttery roast chicken works well with the creaminess of a slightly oaked Chardonnay. Also look for flavours that might clash – very aromatic Gewürztraminer might overpower a simply cooked white fish fillet whereas it would make an Asian-inspired dish of mussels, lime, coconut and lemongrass smile. Under this heading do remember to consider any spicy elements in a dish that can overwhelm a wine.

Quite simply, it is all about the texture, balance and flavour of a wine rather than simply its colour. So, I urge you to gaily abandon outdated rules, such as *white wine only with fish*; they will only prevent you from exploring epicurean heavenly delights, such as Pinot Noir with salmon.

Above all – please experiment and have fun!

My Love of Food and Wine

Somerset in the 1970s could hardly have been called a hotbed of gastronomy. There was certainly great produce, not only the famous cider (although some of it quite lethal and more than one glass best avoided) but also the original home of Cheddar cheese and with great duck, strawberries and dairy products from the Mendips. But the cooking was usually of the meat-and-two-veg variety. Now it abounds with artisan small producers, but back then avocados were still thought exotic (I remember from my childhood the first baked avocado served proudly as a starter – now whatever happened to that recipe?!)

My wonderful mother was – and is – a fabulous cook, and loved to entertain. As children we were often roped in (dressed in jim-jams and dressing gowns, straight from bath time, with still-wet hair making us look deceptively angelic) to go around with the 'nibbles' to accompany the aperitif. So the idea of welcoming friends with food, the love and conviviality that is shared when you get together with people over a meal (no matter how simple or elaborate), was instilled in me from an early age. Combined with school trips to France and visiting pen pals in Holland and Germany, I collected some very different food loves along the way.

Moving to the Cotswolds in my teens ushered in another era of my own food history. Dinner parties were *de rigueur*, with the best crockery, gleaming glassware and three puddings every time! It's also when I developed my love of savoury, rather unconventional breakfasts. Whilst everyone else was keenly devouring their all-butter croissants with apricot conserve, I would be enjoying taramasalata on warm baguette, or Gentleman's Relish (anchovy) on toast topped with Frank Cooper's Oxford Marmalade – still do, much to the shudders of horror from my other half.

I was lucky enough to work between college hours at a friend's deli, which was inspirational. Decorated with reclaimed pews and wooden arched screens from a local deconsecrated church, Shambles was also a vibrant and buzzing café bar. With Edith Piaf and Gypsy Kings wafting through the air, I was immersed in learning about all sorts of foreign cheeses never yet encountered, cute bottles of apricot nectar, Italian pandoro and so much more to seduce me further into the world of food. To confess, my first attempt at making a cappuccino was less than a success (and maybe why I still only drink ristretto or espresso), but my enthusiasm for persuading the good people of Cheltenham into buying whole rounds of Brie de Meaux (at perfect oozing point) was far more effective than my barista skills.

Despite having been lucky enough to have learnt both French and German from the age of six, having fallen in love with Verdi's *La Traviata* I headed off to Italy to learn Italian. After a short but blissful spell in Florence, a wonderful opportunity arose to work in Piemonte for a year. Five years later I was still there, living just outside Turin (the most wonderful city; if you've never been, stop reading right now and go book a flight – or take the overnight train from Paris!).

My passion for Italian food and wine was born and has never left me: lunch at a restaurant whose sole focus was cheese (that had me reeling with amazement many courses and five hours later); the noisy sales calls of stall holders at Turin's marvellous food market in Porta Palazzo (the largest in Europe); the absolute wonder of a truffle hunter and his dog turning up to hunt white truffles in the grounds, the results of which were simply shaved over fried eggs and the delights of learning recipes from my Italian 'family' – nettle risotto was a revelation. I still have my recipe books from that time, painstakingly handwritten either from observing in the kitchen or copied longhand from well-thumbed recipe books. It was here

in Piemonte, not far from the vineyards that produce the world-class wines of Barolo and Barbaresco, that my Pinot Noir-loving palate discovered a new great passion – Nebbiolo. I also fell in love with other grape varieties such as Barbera and Grignolino.

Returning, finally (with a lake of tears shed) to the UK, a short spell at a wine merchant and importer in the North of England taught me so much more about the diversity of wines from around the world – one memorable moment was the first time tasting cool-climate Pinot Noir made by the esteemed winemaker Andrew Pirie from Tasmania. I had great fun at wine fairs, making friends throughout the wine trade (one of the best to be in – we're a friendly bunch!) from Alsace to Burgundy, Portugal to New Zealand.

Falling by chance into my next job took me even further along my exploration of food-and-wine pairing: working for a wine tour company, organising and escorting tours, which meant I was fortunate to meet some of the greatest – and nicest – winemakers out there. I got to work on tour with some of the top names in the English wine trade and Masters of Wines, such as the late Derek Smedley MW, Andrew Jefford, the late Steven Spurrier, Jane Hunt MW, Charles Metcalfe and Victoria Moore to mention only a few. The tours were great fun – also resulting in a great network of friends from regular tour clients (some of whom I saw more often than my own mother!) – from listening to Macbeth being performed in Verona's Roman amphitheatre as the night sky fell, after a hard day's work wine-tasting Amarone, through to Burgundian drinking songs at the Gothic Hospices de Beaune.

As a lover of the sea, I adored being involved in wine cruises aboard beautiful ships such as the legendary windjammer *Sea Cloud*, with her 3,000 square metres (32,000 square feet) of sail. Those hosted for *The Sunday Times* Wine Club provided some of the happiest memories and lifelong friends: Hugh Johnson on board waxing lyrical about Bordeaux; a memorable dinner ashore in a Tuscan vineyard looking down on the ship glittering with lights in the bay below; sailing up the Gironde; and a festival at an organic buffalo farm in Campania.

Starting my own company, Love Wine Food Ltd, was, as such things always are, a leap of faith. I will always be thankful for the unwavering support of friends and family – including those from far-flung wine regions. Social media is not a perfect medium in our society on so many counts, but I will be forever grateful for the technology that allows me to stay in touch with friends and what's going on with vineyards and food producers from Central Otago in New Zealand to Mount Etna in Sicily.

Clients always ask me where my favourite place is to tour – quite impossible to answer! How does one choose from tasting wine against the backdrop of the Dolomites, eating ricotta freshly made in front of you in Campania, travelling the Douro Valley by train, tasting from the barrel at Domaine de la Romanée-Conti, visiting the aging cellars of Culatello to taste their ham and discovering

the delights of Encruzado in Portugal? There are too many wonderful experiences to say. One that has been fascinating is, having taken tours to the vineyards of South America more than twenty times over two decades, watching the vineyards, wines and winemakers of Chile and Argentina – along with Uruguay – develop and really understand and exploit their incredible potential.

To me, food is intrinsically linked with wine, each having the capacity to make the other even better when matched well. Recently I was asked who are the chefs that have inspired me – and this I find quite hard to answer. My intense love (and collection!) of cookbooks is broad and I'm equally inspired by the perfect, simple empañada as by the sheer technical pastry skill of Calum Franklin in *The Pie Book*. It's not so much just about chefs, but the producers who are equally the heroes. But add in food writers and journalists and there are so many people who have unwittingly helped me along my journey into food: *Telegraph* columnist Xanthe Clay, with whom I worked a fun tour in Emilia Romagna with all the deliciousness that involved, from aged balsamic vinegar, seeing Parmesan production and even tasting proper Lambrusco; all the team on *The Food Programme*, of which I am an avid listener, whose forays into the politics of food, as well as simply the taste, are always fascinating and sometimes disturbing; Jay Rayner, whose pithy words are simply brilliant and the late A. A. Gill, whose decadent style of writing, with rapier sharp observations, took me away to so many places without leaving the sofa.

Nigel Slater's books are established favourites on my shelves; he writes so evocatively from *The Christmas Chronicles* to *Toast*. Nigella's repertoire shows strongly, in part for our shared love of all thing's foodie and Italian. There are so many of her simple dishes that play on regular repeat in our kitchen. Jamie Oliver has an incredible range, but again his love of Italy shines though, and will always guarantee to brighten a jaded attitude to 'what's for supper'. Giorgio Locatelli, whose simple respect for great ingredients means that lunch at Locanda Locatelli is always superb.

But also, chefs such as Francis Mallmann, whose food I tasted in Argentina for the first time in the late 1990s – Patagonian lamb, can almost still taste it – and Freddy Bird from Little French in Bristol, whose TV appearances are always guaranteed to bring laughter as much as his food brings smiles of joy. There are so many who have inspired me, it seems wrong just to mention a few – so to the legions not mentioned, I apologise.

Particular cookbooks that are currently – although this changes frequently – splatted with passata and bent slightly out of shape through so much use are: *Venice (Four Seasons of Home Cooking)* by Russell Norman and *The Italian Deli Cookbook* by Theo Randall.

When Slow Food launched in the UK, I was privileged to translate for its president, Carlo Petrini – privileged but also quite nerve-wracked to stand up and free-style translate (Carlo had no notes beyond three words on a scrap of paper) in front of the great and the good of the British food world.

But the philosophy of Slow Food ('Good, Clean and Fair') is something that resonates strongly with me and has led me to discover foods and producers that otherwise I would never have known about.

Getting to know in-depth the local regional foods of Europe and beyond due to my travelling oddly enough bought me closer to seeking out fabulous British foods at home. We now have the most incredible array of British cheeses – just visit Neal's Yard Dairy or I. J. Mellis of Edinburgh for a taster of the huge diversity, from Stichelton, to Evenlode, to Cornish Gouda. Equally delightful is to see the emergence of truly innovative British charcuterie such as Worcestershire wild boar pancetta or Pannage ham from the New Forest.

All the excitement that is surrounding English Wine Production at the moment, combined with wonderful home-produced foods, means this truly is a real golden age of discovery for wine lovers and foodies alike. I hope this book helps in some small way for you to discover the delicious delights on our own doorsteps.

Camel Valley

St. Martin's

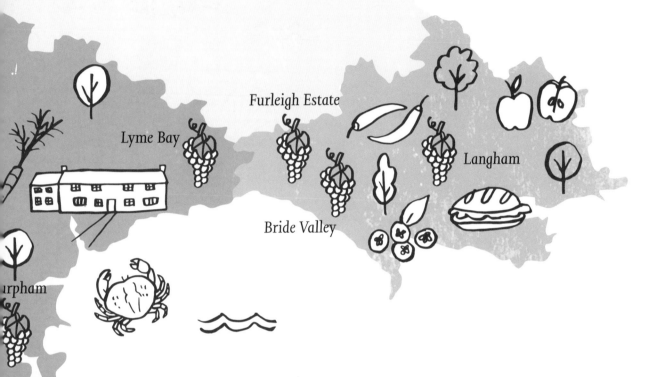

Furleigh Estate

Lyme Bay

Langham

Bride Valley

rpham

CORNWALL,
DEVON
AND DORSET

Welcome to the South West of England, with narrow winding lanes and high hedgerows that lead to picturesque village greens or give tantalising glimpses of the sea before reaching the coast. All three counties are famous for clotted cream – indeed if you ever want to start a heated debate when visiting these beautiful regions, ask a Devonian or a proud Cornish local which goes on top of a scone first – the cream or the jam – and then retreat to a safe distance!

Cornwall – from the moment you cross the Tamar into Kernow, down to its wildest reaches in the Lizard and Land's End, this a land rich in variety, proud of its heritage. This is home to the original Cornish pasty, the wonderfully named stargazy pie eaten on Tom Bawcock's Eve, Fairing biscuits and saffron buns. There's no shortage of places to visit: the dramatic Minack Theatre; St Michael's Mount; the mysterious Lost Gardens of Heligan; the Eden Project (where the annual World Pasty Championships are held) with its biospheres; invigorating surfing on Fistral Beach; the first English tea plantation at Tregothnan; and Falmouth's Oyster Festival. Some of the most inspirational British chefs have put down roots here to take advantage of the spectacular local seafood, including Paul Ainsworth, Nathan Outlaw and Rick Stein.

Devon's small villages endlessly tempt you with cream teas, topped with jam made with wild bilberries from the uplands of Dartmoor; picturesque Clovelly, once famous for its herring fishing, celebrates these silver darlings annually with a festival

(plus a Seaweed Festival); Red Ruby Devon is a local breed of cattle, that gives succulent beef; historic Dartmouth where chef Mitch Tonks weaves his magic on a menu of local sustainable seafood; Plymouth, origin of that naval favourite, Plymouth Gin; eco-campaigner and chef Hugh Fearnley-Whittingstall's famous River Cottage sits close to the Dorset border; the English Riviera of Torquay with its exotic palm trees that feature in Agatha Christie's novels, and her home, Greenway House, overlooking the River Dart. Devon also boasts several places with wonderful food and drink related names: who could resist Guzzle Down, Nutcrackers and Beer?

Dorset, known as Thomas Hardy country, with its fabulous feel of a bygone golden age of seaside holidays, is a county that creeps into your heart without you noticing. It recalls long summer days exploring with the *Famous Five*, whose beloved Kirrin Island was based on Corfe Castle; the classic Dorset apple cake with a generous dollop of clotted cream; mouthwatering sandwiches stuffed with fresh crab, line-caught in Lyme Bay; the annual Great Dorset Chilli Festival for those who like it hot; cockle popcorn at chef Mark Hix's wonderful restaurant in Lyme Regis overlooking the Cobb, made famous in the film *The French Lieutenant's Woman*; the iconic limestone arch of Durdle Door, the fascinating fossils along the Jurassic Coast and the eighteen-mile stretch of shingle at Chesil Beach; the oldest blueberry plantation in England and the headquarters of the incredible Royal National Lifeboat Institution.

CAMEL VALLEY

Almost from its inception, Camel Valley Vineyard has been instrumental in creating a benchmark for quality wines in England. When its owners, Bob and Annie Lindo, first planted vines on their idyllic Cornish estate in 1989, neither of them had any wine background. Through sheer dogged determination, endless graft and an addiction to detail in the vineyards the first wine they entered in a wine competition won a medal. The Lindos' efforts were continually recognised and in 2005 Camel Valley became the first-ever English vineyard to win a Gold Medal at the International Wine Challenge for their *Cornwall* sparkling wine – the only gold awarded to a non-Champagne wine. It is now one of the most well-known of all English sparkling wines.

Since 2002, the winemaking has been taken over by their son Sam, who worked on an estate in New Zealand before returning to the family home in Cornwall, and he has taken the wines to another level. Winemaking is not about chasing medals and trophies, but what an incredible achievement to have the resultant wines so amply rewarded by top judges in blind tastings. Sam has gathered accolades and awards in droves, from becoming UK Winemaker of the Year in 2007 to producing the Best Sparkling Rosé in the World in 2010, ahead of champagne houses Bollinger and Roederer.

Much-loved by leading chefs and restaurateurs alike (Rick Stein and Raymond Blanc are long-time fans), in 2018 Camel Valley was awarded a coveted Royal Warrant – the only English wine to receive this honour. To add to all this, they were also the first English winery to have its own dedicated appellation – PDO of Darnibole Bacchus. Camel Valley's tally of 8,000 vines, including the original vineyard, called Annie's Vineyard (a reference to Sam's mother, who had sole charge of pruning it), has since increased to 30,000. All the winery buildings are solar-powered, in line with the Lindos' aim for sustainability at the estate.

'We always make the style of wine that is most suited to the grapes and climate we have at Camel Valley in Cornwall. We make traditional method sparkling, crisp and aromatic whites and roses. These styles reflect our sense of place and you couldn't make our wines anywhere else in the world.'
Sam Lindo

FEATURED WINE: **Pinot Noir Rosé Brut**. Sam produces an impressive range of wines, both still and sparkling, including the Single Vineyard Darnibole Bacchus, which pairs so well with the mussels and clams grown at Porthilly on the Camel estuary, but his sparkling rosé is also wonderfully food friendly. Redolent of strawberries and fresh zingy red fruit, it is an ideal partner for soft cheeses, a summer fruit pavlova or good old fish and chips!

LOCAL PRODUCE: **Rillettes from Cornish Charcuterie** complement the Camel Valley sparkling wines, or try their pink peppercorn salami to enjoy with the still Camel Valley Rosé, which also goes well with Cornish Gouda.

Riff on Fish & Chips

One of the most classic – and delicious – pairings for English sparkling wine is traditional fish & chips: the perfect supper, preferably eaten whilst sitting on the harbour wall at Padstow, a few miles down-river from the Lindos' vineyards, overlooking the estuary with a glass of Camel Valley fizz in hand. But a slightly more sophisticated recipe seems called for, so here is a Riff on Fish & Chips!

The earthiness of the sweet potatoes, the creamy pistachios and the fresh lemon zest in this dish are all are perfectly balanced with this seductive Cornish sparkling rosé.

SERVES FOUR

2 glugs of olive oil for coating the wedges, plus
    extra for drizzling
2 large sweet potatoes, scrubbed but not peeled
2 tsp ground sumac
4 small slices of white sourdough
120g shelled pistachio nuts
40g mixed soft fresh herbs (parsley, chives, dill,
    tarragon), finely chopped
Zest and juice of 1 lemon
4 thick white skinless fish fillets (MSC cod
    or halibut – or haddock – works well)
4 tbsp Greek yogurt
1 garlic clove, grated

Preheat the oven to 200°C fan/220°C/gas mark 7. Line two baking trays with baking parchment and lightly grease with olive oil.

Slice the sweet potatoes into thin wedges or fat chips. Toss in a bowl with the olive oil and sumac until well coated. Place on one of the lined baking trays in a single layer and bake for 35–40 minutes until tender.

Meanwhile toast the bread and then remove the crusts. When cooled slightly, whizz in a small blender to make fine breadcrumbs. Tip into a bowl then whizz the pistachios until they form a rubble – not too fine. Mix with the breadcrumbs, add the herbs, lemon zest and a drizzle of olive oil.

Place the fish fillets on the second lined tray and coat each one with a tablespoon of Greek yogurt. Carefully press the nut crumb into the yogurt. Don't worry if some of the crumb falls off onto the tray, it will crunch up beautifully.

After the sweet potato wedges have been in the oven for 20 minutes, slide the tray of coated fillets alongside and bake for 12–15 minutes, depending on the thickness of the fillets; use a meat thermometer – the internal temperature of the fish should be 60°C. Serve immediately with the sweet potato wedges.

ST MARTIN'S VINEYARD

The truly spectacular archipelago that forms the Isles of Scilly is located only 28 miles off the coast of Cornwall. Warmed by the Gulf Stream, the islands have long had a reputation for growing flowers and sub-tropical plants. So perhaps unsurprisingly in 1996, some land on St Martin's was converted from flower- to grape-growing. The island boasts incredible white sandy beaches against turquoise seas and is home to a community of just 140 (incredibly lucky!) people.

Following discussions about the vineyard in 2018 with the original owners, in 2020, James Faulconbridge and Holly Robbins took over this boutique vineyard (just 1 hectare), which they work organically, in one of the most southerly reaches of the United Kingdom. The vineyard is located on the coast, near the famous dunes of Par Beach, and is planted with eleven different varieties: Orion, Seyval Blanc, Regent, Rondo, Schönberger, Siegerrebe, Reichensteiner, Madeleine Angevine, Pinots Noir and Meunier and Triomphe d'Alsace. With its present owners' backgrounds in agriculture and ecology, the future of the vineyard looks to be in great hands. St Martin's benefits from a huge biodiversity: James and Holly have bats and swallows, among other visitors, and 140 different wildflower species on their vineyard (and counting…), which contribute to a healthy and resilient soil as well as helping to support a high level of pollinators, such as bees, butterflies and hoverflies – all of which give a balanced ecosystem that minimises the risk of vineyard pests.

Four still wines are produced – a single varietal red from Rondo; a rosé, whose blend is from the Regent variety and also includes some of the infrequently seen Black Homberg; and two white blends – ideal for sipping on a St Martin's beach and whiling away the day.

'Our passion is to create great wine at the same time as managing the vineyard for the diverse flora and fauna that call it home. The vineyard has always been managed in an environmentally sensitive manner — we are moving this further towards an entirely organic and regenerative approach. Seaweed is gathered from the beach after winter storms to fertilise, mulch and control under-vine perennials which, along with a diverse cover crop in the alleys, provides a healthy, nutrient-rich soil. The wind is our greatest challenge in a coastal environment — mimicking the effect of a late frost on the mainland if salt-laced storms blow through when the vines are in flower. After harvest, each variety is fermented individually, and blends are then crafted to complement one another and create unique wines each and every year.'

James Faulconbridge and Holly Robbins

FEATURED WINE: **St Martin's Reserve**. A white blend of Reichensteiner and Siegerrebe. Floral notes, almost the scent of an English hedgerow in summer, with a spicy note coming from the Siegerrebe. There is a touch of salinity in all their wines, thanks to the coastal breezes — very delicate and appealing.

LOCAL PRODUCE: **SC Salt**, made on the island, including a lovely smoked version, is ideal for finishing dishes or even sprinkled on olive oil ice cream.

King Oyster Mushroom 'Scallops' with Pea Purée and Banana Peel Bacon

This recipe is courtesy of the chef of the Seven Stones Inn on St Martin's, Chelsea Quider, whose family owns the Wild Earth vineyard in Central Otago on New Zealand's South Island. James and Holly are vegan and suggested this lovely recipe that Chelsea had cooked for their local supper club. Yes, I can imagine that a few of you will read 'banana peel bacon' and reel in horror or surprise. But bear with me, using the peel, which would otherwise be discarded, has to be good for the eco/green credentials of your kitchen! Plus for those who want a vegan-friendly recipe with a salty, chewy punch – a combination of slightly sweet, slightly smoky – it really does work. If you are not vegan, do still give this recipe a try (you can of course swap in dairy butter or cream as required).

SERVES FOUR

For the Pea Purée:
2 shallots
2 tbsp vegan butter
4 garlic cloves, diced
1 sprig of fresh thyme, plus extra to serve
2 splashes of white wine
500g peas, fresh or frozen
50ml vegan cream (Elmlea, Oatly)
Sea salt and black pepper

For the Banana Peel Bacon:
Marinade ingredients:
   2 tbsp soy sauce
   ½ tsp liquid smoke
   1 tsp paprika
   1 tbsp maple syrup
   ½ tsp garlic powder
   1 tbsp olive oil
2 ripe bananas, preferably organic (ones with lots of brown spots on the skin are ideal)

For the Scallops:
1 shallot, finely sliced
3 garlic cloves, finely diced
200ml white wine
1 tbsp white miso paste
Juice of ½ lemon
1 sheet of nori
500ml vegetable stock
8 king oyster mushrooms
2 tbsp vegan butter

Oil, for frying
Toasted pine nuts, to finish

First make the pea purée. Sauté the shallots in the vegan butter until slightly golden brown, then add the garlic and thyme. Sauté for a few more minutes to let the garlic brown slightly as well.

Splash in the white wine to deglaze the pan, then add the peas and cream. Just warm the peas; do not overcook them or they lose their beautiful green colour. Remove the thyme sprig, transfer to a blender and blend until smooth, adding seasoning to taste.

For the banana peel bacon, mix all the marinade ingredients together in a bowl.

Peel the bananas (save the fruit for another recipe or freeze for smoothies) into 4 nice strips, trim the stalk end and remove any of the white pith from the peel. Soak the peels in the marinade while making the mushroom scallops.

Once almost ready to serve, fry the marinated banana peels in 2 tablespoons oil until very brown and crispy, then remove from the pan and place on kitchen paper to soak up excess oil.

Cut into smaller chunks to sprinkle on top of the scallops before serving.

To make the scallops, heat a glug of oil in a pan and sauté the sliced shallot until translucent. Add in the garlic and continue to sauté for a minute, then add the white wine to deglaze the pan.

Add the white miso paste, lemon juice, nori sheet and vegetable stock and give it a good mix. Bring to a simmer and cover the pan with a lid while preparing the mushrooms.

Cut the mushroom stalks into discs about 2cm thick. (Do not throw the mushroom heads away; keep them for another dish.) Once the mushrooms are all cut, add them to the broth and simmer for 10 minutes, flipping them over halfway through.

After 10 minutes of cooking, transfer the mushrooms to a wire rack to drain slightly.

While your 'scallops' are draining, heat your pan with the vegan butter. Once the pan is hot, add the mushrooms and let them sit for a few minutes to get a nice golden colour, then flip them to colour the other side. Once almost finished, give it all a toss in the pan.

To serve, start by spooning the pea purée on the plate, placing the 'scallops' on top. Sprinkle over the banana bacon bits, scatter with pine nuts, and possibly some fresh thyme sprigs to garnish.

SANDRIDGE BARTON
(HOME TO SHARPHAM WINES)

Sharpham, one of the original trail-blazing estates in the UK, started when Maurice Ash bought the Devon property in the 1960s. The long-term aim was, quite simply, to produce quality wine and cheese in England. As well as raising a herd of Jersey cows, whose rich milk from the lush green pastures made (and still makes) delicious cheeses, Maurice recognised the ideal microclimate of the Dart Valley and in 1981 planted vines. He sold the estate in 1998 to his cousin, current CEO and head winemaker Duncan Schwab, who joined the estate in the 1990s. Duncan has decades of experience of making wines in this idyllic corner of the South West, which shows in the variety and excellence of their range.

Since 2020, Sharpham have been moving their entire cellar operation, lock, stock and barrel (well actually quite a lot of barrels!) across the river to the Sandridge Barton vineyard, which has a limestone ridge, like Burgundy's Côte d'Or. This promises to be exciting with three new hectares planted in 2021, as well as the iron-rich and in parts volcanic soil that already make up their vineyards. The company now takes its name from the south-facing vineyard above the River Dart, though the wines still carry the Sharpham label.

Their wines are generally naturally on the lighter side (around 11–12% ABV) with no manipulation to achieve this – a welcome change from some of today's global wines that tip the scales at almost 15%. Look out for their Wild Ferment Pinot Gris (great with Asian-inspired dishes), their irresistible sparkling rosé, made solely from Pinot Noir (add picnic rug, strawberries, maybe some clotted cream shortbread for the perfect afternoon), or their delicious Madeleine Angevine.

'Despite the new name, we are still the home of Sharpham wine. Same crew, same grapes, same tradition of wines from the Dart Valley. But the addition of this limestone ridge, which is the soil of Burgundy, with these new plantings will mean we can be the English answer to Burgundy.'

Duncan Schwab

FEATURED WINE: **Pinot Noir**. Truly delightful Pinot Noir, which shows greater depth of flavour than some of the newer examples in the UK. This wine, although still delicate in style owing to its cool climate, gives much more complexity with black cherries, hint of violets and black olives as a variety of flavours in the glass.

LOCAL PRODUCE: It has to be one of their own cheeses, so try the **Sharpham Elmhirst**, a rich Vignotte-like cheese – and pour yourself a glass of their Estate Selection white (a Madeleine Angevine and Pinot Gris blend).

Lamb Fillet on Aubergines with Homemade Flatbreads

Pinot Noir and lamb are natural best buddies. Add in garlic, rosemary, as well as fresh clean flavours of parsley and mint, and it is a heavenly friendship. Although this recipe looks quite long, fear not: apart from cooking the lamb, it can be prepared in advance the day beforehand, meaning this is a quick but impressive supper to pair with your Pinot Noir. The flatbreads are inspired by a Paul Hollywood recipe, but I like the lazy no hand-kneading option below. The aubergine dip is similar to the classic Middle Eastern dish, baba ghanoush, and adds a lovely earthiness to the dish as well, which is the natural foil for Pinot Noir. (If really short on time, you could buy some aubergine dip and flatbreads from your local deli – then you will have supper ready almost in the time it takes to lay the table!)

SERVES TWO (BUT EASY TO DOUBLE UP)

Lamb fillets (approx. 300–350g)
A good glug of olive oil, plus extra for frying
2 rosemary sprigs, leaves picked and chopped
4 large sage leaves, chopped
Knob of butter

For the Flatbreads:
250g strong bread flour (wholemeal for preference but white is fine)
5g fine salt
10g sugar
5g quick yeast
15g butter, soft
160ml cool water
Sunflower oil, for greasing and frying

For the Aubergine Dip:
2 large aubergines
1 tsp smoked paprika (optional)
2 tbsp tahini
Juice of 1 lemon, plus possibly a bit extra
35ml olive oil
2 garlic cloves, crushed
2 tbsp each of finely chopped flat-leaf parsley and mint
Sumac and pomegranate seeds, to garnish

The day before you want to devour this delicious recipe, marinate the lamb fillet in the olive oil, rosemary and sage leaves. It's easiest to pop everything in a reusable plastic food bag, massage the meat with the oil and leave in the fridge overnight to marinate.

Make the flatbreads. They keep well, so you can make them the day before or even make ahead and freeze.

Put the flour in the bowl of a stand mixer. Add the salt and sugar to one side and the yeast to the other – this is important as salt kills yeast. Add the butter and water. Using the dough hook, switch the mixer to medium and mix for about 5–8 minutes or until the dough is well combined and silky.

Lightly oil a large ceramic bowl (I use olive oil, but sunflower oil would be fine) and place the dough in the bowl. Cover with a tea towel and leave in warm place to rise (an airing cupboard is ideal). When it has doubled in size – which takes at least an hour but you can leave it for 2–3 hours with no problem – remove the tea towel.

Tip the dough from the bowl onto a floured work surface. Fold the dough inwards and repeat until all the air is knocked out and the dough is smooth. Divide into equal pieces weighing about 60g each and roll into balls. Use a rolling pin to roll each into a round, 20cm across.

Heat a large frying pan over high heat and add 1 tablespoon of sunflower oil. When it smokes (time for the extractor fan usually, hence a good idea to make ahead and reheat), place a dough round in the hot oil and fry for 2 minutes. Flip and cook for a further minute on the other side. Remove and stack on a plate while you cook the rest. Stacking the flatbreads means the steam is trapped between them, so they remain soft. Eat at once or leave to cool for later (they happily last a day under cling film or beeswax food wrap). To reheat simply heat a dry frying pan over a medium heat and warm through for 1½ minutes on each side. They also freeze perfectly but remember to place a sheet of baking paper between them so you can remove one or two at a time.

Make the aubergine dip. First you need to cook the aubergines. Ideally this should be done over an open flame (gas ring or barbecue) to blacken the skin, but as I do not have a gas hob and like eating this on cold January days, I find baking them works just fine. Preheat the oven to 200°C fan/220°C/ gas mark 7. Place the whole aubergines on a baking tray and bake until almost collapsed. This will take about an hour. If in doubt, they probably need longer! Remove and allow to cool. If time permits, I tend to leave in the switched-off oven until cool.

Cut the aubergines in half lengthways and scoop out the soft flesh. If you have patience, you could leave this to drain in a colander for an hour, but if hungry or in a hurry, you can simply squeeze the juices out using a spoon to press the flesh against the sieve. Season and add a bit of smoked paprika if you wish to replicate the smokiness of using a barbecue. Mash gently with a fork.

Mix the tahini, lemon juice and olive oil in a bowl. Stir in the garlic and most of the herbs. Add the mashed aubergine. Taste and add more lemon juice or olive oil if needed. There's no need to be too precise: it's all down to personal taste, so feel free to add more of either as needed! Transfer to a shallow serving dish and sprinkle with sumac.

Remove the meat from the fridge an hour before you are ready to cook. Preheat the oven to 180°C fan/200°C/gas mark 6 and pop in a baking tray to heat up if you don't have an ovenproof frying pan.

Set a large frying pan over a high heat, add a good glug of olive oil and a spoonful of butter. Sear the lamb fillet until coloured and starting to caramelise on the outside, basting as it colours.

Put the lamb into the oven still in the frying pan (if it's ovenproof) or transfer to the preheated baking tray. Cook for 8 minutes for medium-rare, or according to taste.

Remove from the oven, cover with foil and leave to rest for 10 minutes. The fillet should still be pink in the middle but feel free to cook for longer if you prefer. Slice thickly into rounds.

Serve with warm flatbreads, aubergine dip and a bowl of pomegranate seeds. Take a flatbread, layer with aubergine, lamb and pomegranate then wrap, eat and enjoy!

FURLEIGH ESTATE

A stone's throw from the UNESCO World Heritage Jurassic Coast lies this small estate, the brainchild of Ian Edwards and Rebecca Hansford. Planted on a former dairy farm in 2005, they have quickly shown the quality of their wines. They only make wines, both still and sparkling, from grapes grown on their own estate and another vineyard just a mile away to reflect their immediate terroir; none are imported from 'foreign parts' such as Hampshire or Essex.

Like many coming into English wine production from other backgrounds, Ian headed off to Plumpton College in East Sussex, to learn the complexities of winemaking. Such is his aptitude for this new skill, that he was chosen to advise on the wines for renowned wine consultant the late Steven Spurrier, whose estate is in the nearby Bride Valley.

Probably more than any other producer, Furleigh's range of wines caused me the most problems to choose a featured wine. The first I ever tried several years ago was a red blend, Tyrannosaurus Red, aptly named, given their location on this fossil-rich coast. Today they make a white Pinot Noir, a style that is rapidly attracting attention and being made everywhere from Central Otago in New Zealand to Oregon in the Pacific North West of the USA. Their Chardonnay has notes of baked apple and the incredibly popular rosé, Sea Pink, a blend of Pinot Noir and Rondo, has ripe red fruits. My absolute favourite is their top cuvée, From the Oenothèque 10, a vintage sparkling that has seduced many a vintage champagne lover (and English wine sceptic). Do seek it out (worth every penny of its price tag) for its wonderful balance of toasted brioche, almonds and almost savoury finish. But in a bid to show you the diversity of English wines, I plumped for the equally seductive Bacchus Fumé.

FEATURED WINE: **Bacchus Fumé**. Made predominantly from Bacchus, the white variety swiftly becoming the iconic English still white, there is a touch of Chardonnay in the blend, which gives a little more depth to this charming wine. It has beautiful lime notes with tropical fruit balanced so well with beautiful acidity and minerality. Modest but good use of oak ageing has called many a wine journalist in a blind tasting to compare this Bacchus Fumé to a decent Chablis. The lime-rich Kimmeridgean subsoils of Chablis date from the Jurassic age and – like the Thorncombe Sand at Furleigh from the same period – give free-draining soils, ideal for the vine, which really does not like getting its feet wet! Do also look out for Furleigh's rosé, Sea Pink, which is great with summer barbecues as well as the hot smoked eel below.

LOCAL PRODUCE: **Hot smoked eel** from Chesil Smokery in nearby Bridport served with grated carrot and cumin salad and warm soda bread with horseradish butter.

Dorset Crab Rösti

Sat on the Cobb in Lyme Regis, with a soft white bread roll bursting with fresh Dorset crab, that rests easily in my list of top foodie heavens. Lyme Regis even has a whole festival dedicated to these ten-legged crustaceans. One of the strangest things, which I still find unfathomable, is how hard it is to buy spider crab in the UK. They are caught regularly off the South-West coast, with most destined for foreign markets. If you are lucky enough to have a decent fishmonger near you, they should be able to obtain one; otherwise seek out the brilliant W. Harvey & Sons (no relation sadly), shellfish merchants in Newlyn, Cornwall, who offer freshly picked spider crab meat on their website. Failing either of those, there is also the brand Seafood & Eat It, also from Newlyn, and widely available in supermarkets, which has both the brown and white crab meat in one packet.

Chablis is often seen as a default pairing with seafood, and since Furleigh's Bacchus Fumé is in the same flavour/style spectrum this is a terroir triumph in food and wine pairing on home turf.

SERVES FOUR

2 large potatoes (baking potatoes ideal)
1 small onion, thinly sliced
75g brown crab meat
3 tbsp Greek yogurt
Finely grated zest of 1 lemon

Chilli flakes (optional)
100g white crab meat
2 tbsp snipped chives
Rapeseed oil, for frying

To serve:
Large handful of watercress, leaves picked
Olive oil
Dorset sea salt (try their fennel or celery-infused versions)

Peel the potatoes and grate using the large holes on a box grater. Rinse and leave in a colander to drain for 15 minutes. Place in a clean tea towel and wring as much moisture out as possible – be quite tough with it, it's a good stress-busting exercise!

Add the potatoes to a bowl with the onions and season. Using your hands, form into four rösti (flat, fritter-like shapes).

Mix the brown crab meat with the Greek yogurt and finely grated lemon zest and season – add some chilli flakes if to your taste. Mix the white crab meat in a separate bowl with the snipped chives.

Heat a small amount of rapeseed oil in a large frying pan over medium heat. Add the rösti to the pan and squash down slightly to make them thin, vaguely round shapes. When golden and crunchy on one side (about 4–5 minutes but do not let them catch), flip and cook the other side until they are the same colour and crunch.

Plate up one rösti per person. Divide the crab yogurt mix between them and top with the white crab meat and chives. Garnish with the watercress. Drizzle with a flourish of olive oil and dust with flakes of Dorset sea salt.

LYME BAY WINERY

Located in Devon's lovely Axe Valley, Lyme Bay Winery is an innovative company, which has made wonderful English wine since 2013, but for two decades before that date it has been heralded for the award-winning cider and traditional mead made under its parent company name, LBW Drinks.

Unlike other estates featured in this chapter, Lyme Bay source grapes not from their own vines, but from a number of vineyards across the south of England including their home county of Devon as well as Dorset, Hampshire, Essex and Oxfordshire and more. They have long-term relationships with their contract growers, which give them great control over the production and harvesting.

Indeed, the winemakers at Lyme Bay are always looking for ways to experiment, such as their use of sequential inoculation (fascinating for us wine geeks – but don't fret about this technical term… you'll never come across it again!) in the Bacchus mostly sourced from the Essex vineyards with which they have long-term relationships. This type of fermentation gives more layers of flavour and depth to their varietal white wine.

The forward-thinking team at Lyme Bay Winery are keen to promote English still wines not only on the domestic market, successfully placing their wines at competitive prices in carefully selected supermarkets, but also want to realise their potential on the international stage, where currently only sparkling English wines have gained wide recognition. Their long-term strategy is to give their delicious English wines a sustainable future both at home and abroad. Styles range from their classic sparkling through to a still rosé – a blend of three varieties – which is deceptively easy to drink on a summer's day. Although Lyme Bay are very well known for their vibrant whites they are starting to build a reputation for beguiling reds with the arrival of their 2020 still red, a 100% Pinot Noir, with its burst of both red and black fruits on the palate, along with a well-judged amount of oak that does not cover the freshness of the fruit in the glass.

Lyme Bay Winery is a fascinating example of what can be achieved without owning vines. Their work with long-term growers (nothing happens quickly in a vineyard!) allows them to choose the best fruit from the harvest from different regions, which gives their winemaker a greater kaleidoscope of flavours and nuances to play with – a fine balancing act, with so much fruit coming in from such a variety of sources.

'At the Lyme Bay Winery we aspire to make the best wine from the best grapes from the best growers. Our growers excel at planting the right grapes in the right parts of the country to give us amazing fruit to work our winemaking skill upon. We believe this is the best way to start the journey to making world beating wines from England.'

Paul Sullivan, Lime Bay Winery

FEATURED WINE: **Bacchus**. Lyme Bay's varietal Bacchus (they also make a Bacchus blend) really showcases the lively appeal of this grape, rapidly becoming a flagship white variety in England. On the nose it gives lots of lime, with a smidge of ripe tropical fruit hiding in there too. The acidity gives a nervy energy to the wine but has a delightful minerality on the finish.

LOCAL PRODUCE: **Smoked oysters** from River Teign Shellfish Ltd, served with warm buttered baguette is fabulous with Lyme Bay Shoreline, a blend of four white varieties whose crisp citrus notes with an underlying salinity perfectly match the locally caught fish and seafood.

Twice-Baked Goat's Cheese and Wasabi Leaves Soufflé

These are perfectly behaved soufflés, with the second baking giving you, the cook, a comforting reassurance rather than blind panic as guests arrive. Surprisingly perhaps, since wasabi is associated with Japanese cuisine, this type of horseradish is grown in the south of England, and its fresh leaves give a peppery kick to dishes. It is available online but if it is hard to find, here you could instead use chives or watercress leaves (no stems). The citrus notes of the goat's cheese match those in the Bacchus beautifully.

SERVES SIX

50g butter
25g panko breadcrumbs, blitzed briefly in a blender until very fine
40g plain flour
300ml milk, preferably full-fat
150g soft goat's cheese, chopped or crumbled
3 tbsp chopped fresh wasabi leaves (washed and dried thoroughly)
3 large free-range eggs, separated
50ml double cream
30g Parmesan cheese, grated
Sea salt and black pepper

Preheat the oven to 180°C fan/200°C/gas mark 6.

Melt about 10g of the butter in a pan and sparingly brush the insides of six ramekins (approx. size 250ml). Coat the first with panko by rolling the breadcrumbs around until the base and sides are fully coated then tip the rest into the next ramekin and so on.

Melt the remaining butter in the pan over a medium heat. Add the flour and stir to cook for about 2 minutes.

Gradually add the milk – it should be full-fat but as I seldom buy it for one recipe, semi-skimmed works too if that is what you have in the fridge. Stir and gently bring to the boil. Cook for 3–4 minutes until it thickens.

Remove the pan from the heat, add the cheese, wasabi leaves and egg yolks. Beat well, taste and season, bearing in mind that you must slightly overseason to offset the neutrality of the egg whites.

Whisk the egg whites until stiff peaks form. Mix an initial spoonful into the yolk mixture, which helps to blend it, and then carefully fold in the rest using a metal spoon, trying not to knock the air out.

Divide between the ramekins, almost to the top. Run a fingertip around the edge – this gives the soufflé a better chance to rise.

Put the ramekins in a deep-sided baking tray. Fill the tray with boiling water so that it comes halfway up the side of the ramekins. Bake for 15–20 minutes. Remove from the oven and out of the water bath and allow to cool. You can make these ahead at this point and keep in the fridge for baking later or the following day.

When you are ready to serve, preheat the oven to 200°C fan/220°C/gas mark 7. Run a round-bladed knife around the inside edge of the soufflés and turn out into a buttered ovenproof dish. You can do this in individual dishes or a larger ceramic serving bowl.

Pour the cream over the top, sprinkle with the Parmesan and bake for 10 minutes. Serve at once, possibly with a simple watercress salad on the side.

BRIDE VALLEY

Founded by Arabella and Steven Spurrier, this boutique estate of just ten hectares nestles in the beautiful Bride Valley in west Dorset. For many wine lovers, the name of Steven Spurrier, who sadly died in 2021, is more associated with either France or California. The quintessential, ever-dapper English gentleman, Steven owned a wine shop in Paris, from where he launched what became a world-changing wine competition, the so-called 'Judgment of Paris', in 1976, where California wines triumphed over iconic and classic French wines in a blind-tasting. An illustrious career in wine ensued for Steven, travelling, teaching, consulting, judging and commenting on wines across the globe.

The Spurriers bought a property in Litton Cheney in Dorset in 1987 where Bella kept sheep until they realised that their south-facing slopes and chalky soils would be ideal for making sparkling wine. They established vines on root stocks from Guillaume, at Charcenne, one of the most revered nurseries in Burgundy, and today their Bride Valley estate is planted with the three classic sparkling varieties: Chardonnay, Pinot Noir and Pinot Meunier. Combining Steven's extensive wine knowledge and Bella's focus on sustainability, their vision was realised: their first harvest, 2011, was released in 2014. Bella runs the vineyard, with their vineyard manager Graham Fisher, and the grapes are vinified by Ian Edwards at the neighbouring Furleigh Estate.

'We call this crémant "a wine of necessity" for the following reasons. The year 2015 was not good, producing acidic grapes with very low alcohol. We made a little Sparkling Rosé, and left the rest in tank, hoping for better in 2016. It was better, but still not great, so we blended the two, producing our first non-vintage. However, Steven was still dissatisfied. He asked the winemaker, Ian Edwards, of Furleigh Estate, "can you make me a Cremant?" His reasoning being that the lighter sparkle of the Cremant would soften the wine, making it more approachable. It worked a treat!

   The crémant will always be marketed as a non-vintage, though the current [as of 2022] batch is in fact 2018, a splendid year for all English wine; would that there were more like it. Our quirky climate means that that our winemakers and growers need to employ quick thinking and adaptability sometimes... hence the crémant. A wine of necessity, and still the only one in England!'
Bella Spurrier

FEATURED WINE: **Dorset Crémant**. Although the estate produces four delightful sparkling wines and three still ones, including an enticing Pinot Noir rosé, the crémant was chosen as a truly ideal aperitif wine. The appreciation of crémant as a style is hugely on the increase among lovers of bubbles. It is made with the same secondary fermentation in bottle as the champagne method, but which results in a lower pressure than other sparkling wines, culminating in gentler bubbles and making it extremely easy to enjoy a second glass of crémant! At this time little crémant is produced in the UK, which makes the delicate, creamy flavours and crisp green apple notes of the Bride Valley example all the more delightful.

LOCAL PRODUCE: **Smoked Blyton**, created by the brilliantly named Book & Bucket Cheese Company in Dorset, is a delicious smoked, brie-style cheese with lovely mushroomy notes that marries perfectly with Bride Valley Blanc de Blancs, which, with its delightful balance of green apples and a long smooth finish, Steven considered to be Bride Valley's signature wine.

Cheese Sablé Biscuits

Although the crémant happily matches fish dishes — everything from fish & chips to baked salmon fillets, it shines as an aperitif — and these small sablé biscuits are an ideal accompaniment. Look out for beetroot and apple-infused sea salt from the Dorset Sea Salt Company for its earthy flavour.

MAKES ABOUT 20

175g plain flour, plus extra for dusting
Generous pinch of Beetroot & Apple Sea Salt,
    plus extra for dusting ½ tsp English mustard
    powder
½ tsp smoked paprika
1 tsp ground cumin

150g salted butter, chilled and diced
75g Comté cheese (or similar textured cheese),
    finely grated
75g pecorino (or similar textured cheese),
    finely grated (plus a little extra for topping)
A little milk, for glazing

Put the flour, sea salt, mustard powder, paprika and cumin into a mixing bowl. Add the butter and rub into the dry ingredients with your fingertips.

Add the grated cheeses and rub together again until a dough starts to form — you may need a tiny amount of cold water.

Put the dough onto a floured work surface and roll into a log about 5cm in diameter. Wrap in clingfilm and chill in the fridge for 2 hours to firm up.

Preheat the oven to 160°C fan/180°C/gas mark 4. Line a flat baking sheet with baking parchment.

Take the dough from the fridge and unwrap. Slice into biscuits about 5mm thick.

Place on the baking tray, spaced apart.

Brush lightly with milk and sprinkle over pecorino cheese and sea salt.

Cook for 12–15 minutes until golden. Remove from the oven and allow to cool on the sheet.

Note: These sables keep well in a tin for 3–4 days but you can also freeze the uncooked dough, sliced and layered with greaseproof paper, so you have a batch on standby for unexpected guests. You can cook from frozen — add about 3–4 minutes to the cooking time but keep an eye on them in the oven.

LANGHAM WINE ESTATE

Owner Justin Langham, an arable farmer and lover of good wines, was thinking about diversification of crops, when he took inspiration from the fact that his father, John, had planted some vines at their beautiful Dorset property, Melcombe Manor. The Langham estate was established in 2009 when Justin planted twelve hectares on a single site on their nearby Crawthorne Farm. Their philosophy has always been to produce a style of wine that reflects its terroir, made with minimal intervention as possible. The enthusiasm of winemaker Tommy Grimshaw, currently one of the youngest head winemakers in the UK, is obvious. He creates layers of flavours using natural yeasts and a range of used French oak barrels, which give structure and micro-oxygenation to the wine without overdominating the flavour profile of the fruit with oak influence.

Recognition of this quality came in 2020, with Langham beating leading champagne houses in the International Wine and Spirit Competition (IWSC), the world's largest and most influential competition for wines. To take the trophy from more than 700 entries was quite a coup for an English sparkling wine.

'The IWSC "Sparkling Wine Producer of the Year" accolade in 2020 was fantastic for us in so many ways. Customers, press and the trade now take us as far more serious players, which although we always thought we were, it was often difficult getting this message across. However, we must not rest on our laurels, as it might be easy to do. We must continue to strive to create the most interesting wines we possibly can and always be open to new ideas and techniques, which I know our small young team wish to do too.'
Justin Langham

FEATURED WINE: **Blanc de Blancs**. Langham is dedicated to the production of quality sparkling wines using the traditional method of secondary fermentation in bottle, and the featured 100% Chardonnay fizz shows bags of complexity. It has all the expected notes of freshly made toast but, importantly and very appealingly, these are balanced by a kick of pure linear acidity, which makes it an excellent match for seafood, cream and pastry. Look out too for Langham's sparkling made solely from Pinot Meunier grapes – something of a rarity – as this variety is usually blended with Pinot Noir.

LOCAL PRODUCE: **Truffle Wordsworth**, also made from the team at the fabulously named Book & Bucket Cheese Company, has the intense style of a Gouda, but with added black summer truffles, which mirror so well the Chardonnay of the Blanc de Blancs.

Scallop Pies

On a wonderful, memorable, though slightly busman's holiday, visiting the fabulous vineyards of Tasmania, we fell in love with these irresistible scallop pies. The rich buttery pastry encasing a creamy slightly spicy filling is a heavenly foil for the richness of the Langham Blanc de Blancs, with the bubbles and acidity lifting the buttery pastry.

Succulent scallops are caught all around British shores, but please do look out for sustainably caught scallops – those that are hand dived – not dredged, which destroys the seabed and so much other marine life (check out the Pesky Fish company).

MAKES FOUR PIES

12 medium scallops or 24 small 'queenie' scallops
    (fresh or frozen, with or without roe)
240ml fish stock
Juice of ½ lemon
4 tbsp double cream
3 egg yolks
2 tbsp butter
1 tsp medium curry powder (Australian Keen's
    Curry Powder, if you can find it)
2 tbsp plain flour
2 tbsp chives, finely chopped
1 tsp lemon zest
1 tbsp olive oil
1 sheet readymade shortcrust pastry
1 sheet readymade all-butter puff pastry

Make sure your scallops are clean or fully defrosted and keep them in the fridge until needed. (You can choose to use the roe or not according to your taste.) Gently warm the fish stock and keep at a low simmer.

Meanwhile, whisk together the lemon juice, cream and two of the egg yolks in a large jug. Melt the butter in a saucepan over a medium heat and, when foaming, add the curry powder and stir in the flour. Cook, stirring, for 1 minute. Slowly whisk in the hot stock and bring to the boil. Simmer for 2 minutes then add one-third of the hot sauce to the egg yolk mixture, stirring all the time. Pour the mixture into the pan of hot sauce, lower the heat and stir constantly until the eggs cook and thicken the sauce. Taste, season and add the chives and lemon zest. Remove from the heat and set aside while you cook the scallops.

If not using queenies, cut the scallops into bite-sized pieces. Heat the olive oil in a small frying pan and sear the scallops, in batches, on both sides. Transfer to a large bowl and allow to cool. When they are cool, spoon over the sauce to create a thick mixture. Put in the fridge to chill for 1 hour.

Unroll the pastry sheets and use a cookie cutter to stamp out four circles from the shortcrust sheet large enough to line four holes of a muffin pan, then cut out four lids from the puff pastry. Put the latter back in the fridge.

Preheat the oven to 200°C fan/220°C/gas mark 7. When the scallop mixture is fully chilled, fill the pastry cases almost to the rim (you may not need all the sauce). Beat the remaining egg yolk and brush it over the edges of the pies then cover with the puff pastry lids and pinch/crimp to seal. Glaze the lids with egg yolk.

Bake for 10 minutes then reduce the temperature to 180°C fan/200°C/gas mark 6 and cook for a further 20 minutes.

Leave the pies to stand for 5 minutes before serving.

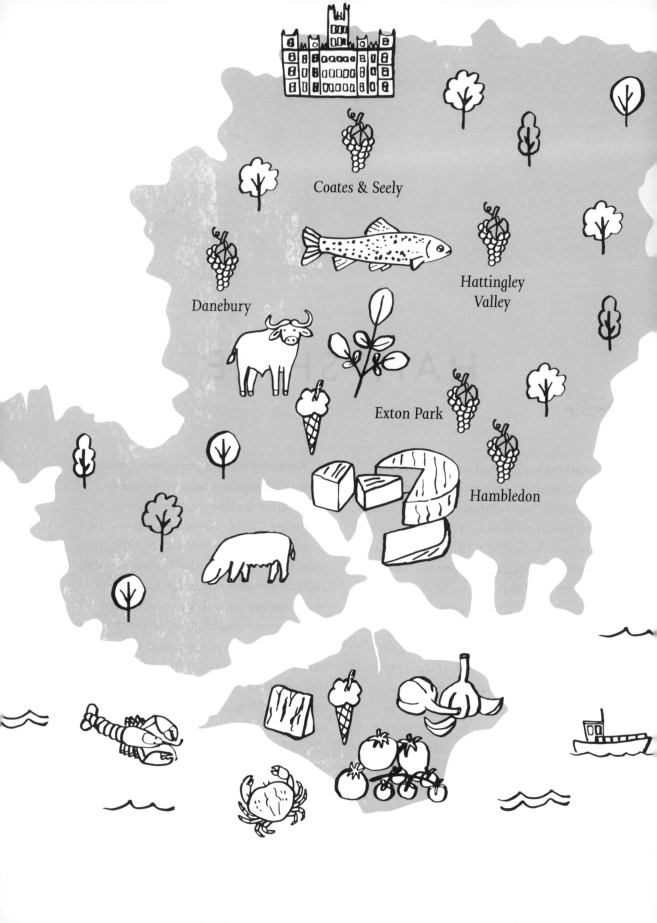

Coates & Seely

Danebury

Hattingley
Valley

Exton Park

Hambledon

HAMPSHIRE

Hampshire, on England's south coast is a glorious medley of coast and countryside, with small villages and market towns dotted across the South Downs. A mere four miles offshore is the beautiful Isle of Wight, famous for its Garlic Festival, flavoursome heritage tomatoes, IOW blue cheese, Minghella ice cream, Mermaid gin, a Round the Island yacht race and one of Queen Victoria's favourite residences, Osborne House. On the mainland the crystal-clear chalk streams of the River Test, a favourite of anglers, are home to slow-grown trout as well as watercress – a crop once so important it had a dedicated railway, the Watercress Line, where steam trains still run. In the valley of the Test, water buffalo are raised by former Formula One racing world champion, Jody Scheckter. Their milk makes simply the best ice cream – as well as glorious mozzarella.

Known as Jane Austen's county, more recently Hampshire become famous as the location for *Downton Abbey* (filmed at Highclere Castle). The ancient oaks of the New Forest, which dates back to 1079, are ideal foraging for pigs that roam under the trees for the annual pannage, joining the disdainful ponies and donkeys on forest roads to assert their right of way over visiting tourists; Winchester, the county town, previously the Capital of ancient England and seat of King Arthur and Knights of the Round Table; the cradle of cricket; the Neo-classical mansion that hosts The Grange Opera Festival; sailing on the River Hamble and Solent; and production of award-winning artisan cheeses Tunworth and Winslade.

DANEBURY VINEYARDS

Truly a boutique-sized estate at just three hectares, Danebury Vineyards is tucked away down leafy lanes, close to the picturesque town of Stockbridge in the Hampshire Downs. This family-owned English vineyard is run by a small team producing both still and sparkling wines in a distinctly English style of floral hedgerow notes. The rock at Danebury Vineyards is chalk and flint, with a thin covering of topsoil – ideal for vines – and forms part of the same geological seam that lies beneath the Channel and pops up again in the Champagne region.

In Victorian times, the property was a famous racing stable yard, accommodating the racehorses of the nobility who raced at the local racecourse. Indeed, their flagship vintage brut sparkling wine, Cossack, is named after a Derby winner trained at Danebury. The vineyard was the paddock for the racing stable – they still dig up the occasional Victorian horseshoe!

Vines were planted in 1988 with the ethos of working with nature, and continue to be a traditional mix of white varieties: Auxerrois Blanc and Ruländer (otherwise known as Pinot Gris) for the Cossack sparkling, and Madeleine Angevine and Schönburger for varietals (single-grape wines) that display a floral elegance and delicate flavours. The Reserve shows masterful blending of their four grape varieties. Production at Danebury is small, but it is fascinating to be able to taste these less-mainstream varieties, which do so well on these flint and chalk soils.

'Our focus is to produce elegant, well-balanced wines in small batches with minimal intervention in the vineyard and winemaking.'

Patrick Westropp, Estate Manager

FEATURED WINE: **Madeleine Angevine**, a white variety that originally hails from France's Loire Valley, has really made its home at Danebury where it reveals enticing floral notes combined with crisp red apples and hedgerow flowers. It sits happily alongside most seafoods as well as the prized trout from the nearby River Test.

LOCAL PRODUCE: **Old Winchester Cheese**, on its own or made into cheese sablé biscuits. Also, not far from Danebury, is Parsonage Farm Charcuterie, which makes a fabulous range of British charcuterie, including a lemon, fennel seed and black pepper coppa. Either the cheese or the cured meat are ideal with a glass of Danebury Cossack Sparkling.

Clam Fregola

Watercress has been grown in Hampshire for centuries. A handful of its peppery leaves lifts even further the pairing of fragrant white wine with the iodine-infused minerality of this shellfish dish.

Fregola is a type of Sardinian pasta with a nutty flavour made from either wheat or semolina flour. The small beads are usually made by hand, which gives a wonderful irregularity. It's also known as Sardinian couscous and, although it's not the same, if you cannot find fregola, you could use giant couscous instead.

SERVES FOUR

1kg fresh small clams
Olive oil, for frying
150ml dry white wine
2 garlic cloves, crushed
Large handful of watercress, chopped
250g fregola
200g passata (or use ½ can of chopped tomatoes)

Wash the clams and put in a large clean bowl with salted water. Leave for 1 hour. Rinse very well under running water and drain.

Heat 2 tablespoons olive oil in a large, lidded frying pan over a medium heat. Add the clams and the wine. Cook with lid on for about 3–4 minutes, shaking the pan occasionally – this helps the clams to open.

Remove from the heat and shell most of the clams, leaving a couple of handfuls still in their shell for the final dish.

Strain the cooking liquid (including any clam juice) through a fine sieve and put aside.

Heat 2 generous glugs of olive oil in a large saucepan with the crushed garlic. Scatter in most of the watercress and stir well into the oil.

Add the fregola and stir to toast the grains for a minute. Pour in the clam cooking juice and the passata or tomatoes. Cook the fregola over a medium heat according to the packet instructions or until soft but still with bite. (If the pan looks dry, you can add in some fish stock or hot water.)

When the fregola is cooked, stir in the shelled clams, and heat through for a minute or two.

Serve in warm pasta bowls, topped with the clams still in their shells and the rest of the chopped watercress.

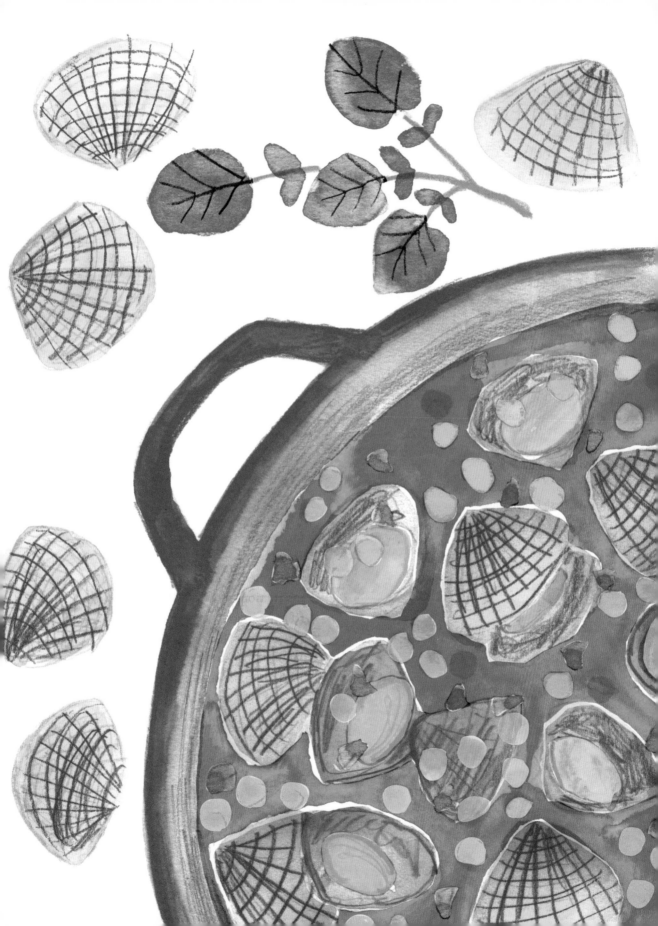

COATES & SEELY

This estate is the embodiment of the dream of two close friends, Nicholas Coates and Christian Seely, to make sparkling English wine that could stand proud and equal to the best in the world. They chose a secluded valley close to the River Test where the thin chalk soils of the south-facing slopes were deemed ideal for their bid to make outstanding fizz.

Across their six wines, there is a recognisable style: carefully managed acidity, beautifully balanced with seductive complexity and absolute style. These are wines designed to be enjoyed with friends and good food, possibly on a leisurely Sunday afternoon on the riverbank, in the style of a *Wind in the Willows* picnic.

Nicholas's wife, Virginia, creates wonderful food pairings for their wines. Her enthusiasm for good food was inherited from her White Russian grandmother, before she went on to train as a chef at Leith's. Nicholas runs the day-to-day business, displaying an inspiring attention to detail for every aspect of the estate, with regular visits from Christian who is based in France, where he is head of the prestigious wine estates owned by the AXA Millésimes group, which include the illustrious Château Pichon Baron in Pauillac, Bordeaux, and the revered Port estate of Quinta do Noval in the heart of the Douro Valley.

Coates & Seely have their own approach to tackle the thorny subject of what to call English sparkling wine, simply labelling their version as *Britagne*, and made by the *Méthode Britannique* — slightly tongue-in-cheek names with which to gently tease our winemaking friends on the other side of the Channel. Obviously they are not an issue, as the C&S wine is the only English wine to enjoy a listing at the prestigious Hôtel George V in Paris!

If you are spending a day at the races, at Epsom, Sandown or Newmarket racecourses, do look out for their classic 1952 vintage coach, Albion, decked out in racing green, always ready to dispense a glass of excellent bubbles.

'Our wines combine traditional winemaking craftsmanship, modern technology, and an endless pursuit of excellence, and seek above all to express the unique character and beauty of our English chalk terroir.'

Nicholas Coates

FEATURED WINE: **La Perfide Vintage Rosé 2009**. Although I've selected the La Perfide, any of the C&S wines would happily be my companion if I were left on a desert island – for example their NV Rosé is perfect with a bowl of raspberries and the Blanc de Blancs is heaven with black olive palmiers – their top rosé cuvée, La Perfide 2009 is outstanding. The five years ageing on the lees, as well as in bottle, results in a wine with incredible suavity and great length.

About 90% Pinot Noir and the rest Pinot Meunier, this is a serious rosé that ages gracefully and is wonderfully food friendly, happy with everything from tuna carpaccio to guinea fowl.

LOCAL PRODUCE: Hampshire-made **Tunworth**, rated 'the best camembert in the world' by Raymond Blanc, is heaven with the C&S Brut Reserve NV.

Smoked Trout, Courgette and Watercress Roulade

Hoping that you do not turn over the page at the mention of a roulade, please trust me – they are super-simple to make. Any slight cracks from rolling can always be hidden under whipped cream, a grating of cheese or a bunch of herbs placed with a confident flourish! Perhaps you think that they are too 1980s but such is my belief in the low effort:high impression ratio of a roulade, I have included two in this book: one savoury, one sweet. Well, once you have discovered how easy they are, you will need a second recipe to try!

Virginia Coates, co-owner and Head of Events at C&S is a Leith's-trained chef and she generously cooked my recipe here, and commented on the matching with the C&S wine: 'I have cooked it, it's delicious, simple to make and is a great use of local fabulous Chalk Stream Trout!'

Do look out for smoked trout under the label ChalkStream. The farms that supply the company slow-grow trout in the crystal-clear chalk streams in Hampshire, where Coates & Seely are based. Either their hot or cold smoked trout works well with this recipe. The delicate pink flesh is sublime with the impressive rich rosé, with its multi-layered flavours.

SERVES SIX

500g courgettes, coarsely grated (in season, a mix of yellow and green looks pretty)
25g butter, plus extra for greasing
2 shallots, finely chopped
250g fromage frais
25g Parmesan, grated
4 tbsp fresh soft breadcrumbs
3 large free-range eggs, separated
250g soft cream cheese
3 tsp creamed horseradish
4 tbsp chopped watercress leaves, plus extra sprigs to garnish
250g smoked trout fillets, flaked
Sea salt and black pepper

Mix the grated courgettes with a teaspoon of fine salt and leave to drain in a colander for 1 hour.

Preheat the oven to 190°C fan/210°C/gas mark 7. Butter and base-line a Swiss roll tin (or a 25 × 33cm baking tray) with baking paper.

Rinse the courgettes and, using a clean kitchen cloth or tea towel, wring out as much moisture as possible – be quite assertive about this.

Melt the butter in a large frying pan and fry the shallots until soft (about 6 minutes). Stir in the courgettes. Cook for a further 5 minutes, stirring often. Season and set aside to cool.

When fully cool, combine with the fromage frais, parmesan, breadcrumbs and egg yolks.

In a scrupulously clean bowl, whisk the egg whites until stiff peaks form. Mix a spoonful of this into the courgette mixture and stir to incorporate. Using a metal spoon, very gently fold in the rest of the whites into the mixture, keeping in as much air as possible. Pour into the lined tin and smooth level. Bake for 15–20 minutes until the centre of roulade is just firm.

Meanwhile, make the filling. Beat the cream cheese with a spoon until smooth then add horseradish to taste. Beat in the chopped watercress. Season.

Put a clean tea towel on the work surface and cover with a sheet of baking paper. Turn out the roulade onto this paper. Remove the lining paper and trim the edges of the roulade. Using the tea towel to help you, roll up the (unfilled) roulade from one short side, with the sheet of paper inside. Leave to cool and then unroll.

Gently spread the cream mixture across the unfurled roulade, cover with trout and reroll (without the paper!). Garnish with sprigs of watercress. Cut into thick slices and serve.

EXTON PARK

With more than a quarter of a century of intense vineyard wandering around the world under my belt, I've been lucky enough to see some stunning views. But my first visit to Exton Park still took my breath away. During a recce tour around their estate in a 4x4, hosted by the eloquent MD Kit Ellen, the view from the top of their sixty-acre single vineyard across the Meon Valley in Hampshire was quite simply heart-stoppingly beautiful.

Exton Park's creation was thanks to Malcolm Isaac MBE, who after regenerating the English watercress trade (once so important in Hampshire that a dedicated train line was built to transport the crop of this healthy superfood to London), went on to revolutionise the entire British salad industry. He bought the Exton Park estate in 2009 and planted eight hectares with vines. Still involved today, albeit not quite so hands on, but always popping in, his vision for creating fabulous wines from this relatively young English vineyard is one shared by the tightly knit team that runs the estate. In charge of the vineyards is Fred Langdale, whose passion was rewarded in 2020 with a Nuffield Scholarship allowing him to continue his research into cool-climate vineyards.

One of the key decisions was to hire Corinne Seely as wine director. Some of the most outstanding winemakers I have met across the world are female, so it must simply be her charming, decidedly French accent that still raises a few eyebrows on first encounter: a French winemaker at an English estate!?! Corinne's wide experience of making wine began in Bordeaux at a highly regarded Graves *grand cru classé* estate, Domaine de Chevalier. At Exton the focus has been to build a ten-year library of reserve wines by keeping back wine from each year's harvest. This gives Corinne a breadth and depth of different flavour profiles to create their Reserve Blend wines from different vintages, giving a consistency of style. The reserves all spend at least three years in bottle before being released.

In October 2021 their three Reserve Blends were joined by RB45 Blanc de Blancs (the 45 refers to the number of library wines used in the final blend), which I tasted as a preview sample in summer 2021. It was a fabulous glass of bright, elegant complexity that continued to reveal layer upon layer of flavours. At this lovely site, they have also recently opened Exton Hall – a marvellous place to discover their wines, including private events with guest chefs to pair their wines with a variety of cuisines.

'I do not want to make a copy of champagne. England is a new category of wine – a new challenge and adventure.'
Corinne Seely

FEATURED WINE: **Exton Park RB23 Rosé**. A blend of Pinots Noir and Meunier, this sparkling rosé not only bursts with all the fresh English summer fruits but has a delightful salinity on the finish.

LOCAL PRODUCE: **Twisted Nose Gin** made by Winchester Distillery – using watercress to give a pepperiness as well as nine other locally grown botanicals. Oh, and do look out for the annual Alresford Watercress Festival to celebrate all things watercress!

Watercress Scones

There was no question that for Exton Park, the recipe simply had to include watercress, to honour Malcolm's association with the local production and this recipe was given to me by a Hampshire watercress grower I met at a local farmer's market. Watercress has been a very important crop in the county since the early 1800s, as an easy source of various nutrients and vitamins. The industry's hub was the small Georgian town of Alresford and a dedicated train route, the 'Watercress Line', was established to transport the watercress to London (these days the steam train is back in service as a tourist route).

Old Winchester is a multi-award-winning hard cheese, reminiscent of Gouda, made on Lyburn Farm in the New Forest by the Smales family using milk from their Friesian herd. The rennet used is vegetarian, making the cheese a veggie-friendly alternative to Parmesan for grating. Old Winchester is delicious eaten on its own; the curd is washed, giving it a sweet tang and the ageing for about 18 months produces wonderful crystals in the cheese.

Here, the method is for making the dough by hand but if you choose to use a stand mixer, just be careful not to overwork it.

MAKES NINE SCONES

100g watercress (washed and fully dried)
225g self-raising flour, plus extra for dusting
2 tsp baking powder
1 tsp English mustard powder or wasabi powder
A pinch of salt
50g cold butter, cubed
75g Old Winchester cheese (or Cheddar if preferred)
200ml buttermilk (plus a little extra for glazing)

Preheat the oven to 200°C fan/220°C/gas mark 7. Line a large baking sheet with baking paper (or, if your sheet is non-stick, simply dust with flour).

Finely chop the watercress, discarding only very woody stalks.

Sift the flour, baking powder, mustard and salt into a large bowl. Add the cubed butter and rub in with your fingers until it forms breadcrumbs.

Add the chopped watercress and two-thirds of the grated cheese and mix. Make a well in the centre and add the buttermilk. Use a round-bladed knife to combine the mix into a soft dough before lightly kneading on a surface dusted with flour.

Roll out the dough to about 2.5cm thick. Use a 6cm pastry cutter to cut out nine rounds (you may need to regather and lightly reroll the dough).

Place the scones on the baking sheet. Brush with a little buttermilk and scatter with the remaining cheese. Bake for 20–25 minutes or until golden. Leave to cool for at least 5 minutes – they are irresistible warm.

Serving suggestion: Slather warm scones with cream cheese mixed with chopped pieces of oak-smoked tomatoes (use some of the oil, too) from the Tomato Stall on the Isle of Wight – just across the Solent from mainland Hampshire!

HATTINGLEY VALLEY

Nestled at the end of a leafy Hampshire country lane, the impressive cellar set-up at Hattingley Valley comes as a bit of a surprise. It's been home since 2010 to one of the most influential winemakers in the UK. Emma Rice has been weaving her magic on the Hattingley wines using not only their own grapes but also sourcing some from growers across the south of England. This gives her a wider range of flavours to work with in final blends because even within the same grape variety, Chardonnay grown in, say, Essex will give her a different flavour profile from one grown in, say, Somerset. The practice also minimises their risk factor – always a consideration with the English weather – if the crop in one area of the country is affected by frost or hail, for example. As well as all this, Emma also makes wines for several other English wine estates, hence the spacious cellar facilities at HV. She has also won UK Winemaker of the Year award – twice!

Hattingley Valley's owner, Simon Robinson, has long been a passionate promoter of the wines of England in general, not just those from his own estate. Interestingly, if proof were needed of the quality at Hattingley, its winemaking facilities were chosen for the first English sparkling by leading French champagne house Pommery, released in 2018.

The Hattingley Classic non-vintage sparkling wine has a delightful purity of nervy acidity balanced with a judicious amount of oak for structure. But do also seek out their flagship fizz, Kings Cuvée, with its opulent style from its 100% barrel fermentation and ageing in old French oak barrels combined with a low dosage that keeps the acidity singing. Hattingley also have been instrumental in flying the flag of English wines abroad, with just over a third of their business heading for export markets, including their delicious Provençal-style still rosé from Pinots Noir, Précoce and Meunier.

'Our focus has always been sparkling wine, with still wines only considered in exceptional circumstances. The Entice was our first still wine and it is one of our most popular. The method of freezing the grapes means that we can only make small volumes and we can't do it every year – the Bacchus has to be sufficiently ripe – but it is indicative of our innovative approach at Hattingley. We now make a wider range of Still by Hattingley as and when vintage conditions allow.'
Emma Rice

FEATURED WINE: **Entice Dessert Wine.** One common characteristic of all great winemakers is the desire to experiment and no less so than at Hattingley where, alongside their still wines and fizz, they also make an intriguing dessert wine – Entice. Only four times in the company's short history has this unusual wine been produced in vintages where the sugars show the potential for concentrating. Made purely from Bacchus grapes that have been frozen, it is similar in style to an ice wine. Lots of lovely, honeyed notes as well as the classic vibrant varietal notes of elderflower, with peardrop and ripe stone fruits. Although it naturally pairs with a host of desserts, it also works well with pâté or with blue cheese as in the recipe overleaf.

LOCAL PRODUCE: **Red Fox Cheese Soufflé** – made in nearby Stockbridge. Buy ready prepared and simply heat, so no worries about collapsing soufflés. Simultaneously light and rich, this is ideal with the Kings Cuvée.

Stichleton Bruschetta with Roasted Apricots and Thyme

225g Stichelton cheese
250g tub of ricotta
4 ripe apricots, halved and stoned
Small handful of fresh thyme, leaves picked
Honey (runny and, if possible, dark such as chestnut honey)
Olive oil, for drizzling
4 slices of Pugliese bread
Salt and freshly ground black pepper

It might seem strange to match a dessert wine with bruschetta, but so often sweet wines taste unbalanced due to the intense sweetness of the pudding – and the Entice wine goes superbly with blue cheese. (I did toy with the idea of matching it with blue cheesecake with a base of gingernuts, which worked well, but the Bruschetta won by a smidge.) This makes a great light lunch with some dressed leaves, or a starter – it's even been known to appear instead of a dessert or cheese course.

The texture and crumb of Pugliese bread is perfect for bruschetta, and the Crosta & Mollica brand is widely available, but any decent sourdough would work well here – or perhaps even a walnut bread. Stichleton is the unpasteurised version of Stilton, which gives it a creamy, more delicate taste than Stilton – but you could easily swap if you cannot find Stichelton.

SERVES FOUR

Take both cheeses out of the fridge an hour before you start.

Preheat the oven to 180°C fan/200°C/gas mark 6 and line a baking tray with baking paper. Place the apricots cut side up on the lined tray, scatter with half the thyme leaves and drizzle with runny honey. Bake for about 20–25 minutes until tender, when a small knife slides in easily, and the tops have a dark caramelised colour.

Meanwhile, in a bowl crumble the Stichleton into the ricotta, tasting as you go until you have right depth of flavour – you might not need all the blue cheese. Beat with a spoon until lightly mixed. Drizzle in some olive oil if needed to mix better. Season.

Toast the bread on each side – a griddle pan is ideal to get the cute lines but under a grill is also fine. Spread with the cheese mixture, top with the warm apricots, a final drizzle of honey and olive oil, plus the rest of the thyme leaves and serve.

HAMBLEDON VINEYARD

One of the most recognisable of all English wine estates (their beautiful vineyards in the South Downs National Park appear atop many a magazine article about English wines) Hambledon is the oldest commercial vineyard in England. The original site in the small village of Hambledon in Hampshire's Meon Valley was planted in 1952 with advice from the esteemed Champagne house of Pol Roger. The estate underwent a renaissance when it was purchased by Ian Kellett in 1999, his decision to focus solely on sparkling wines visionary given the cool-climate, south-facing slopes and geology of the South Downs.

The classic Champenoise varieties of Chardonnay, Pinot Noir and Pinot Meunier are made into four different cuvées at the estate, under the careful eye of winemaker Félix Gabillet, overseen by Hervé Jestin, a wine consultant and renowned former *chef de cave* at Champagne Duval Leroy. Hambledon feature their Classic Cuvée, both white and rosé, the latter aged for a minimum of 45 months before release. Both are great wines for an aperitif. But their flagship wine is their Première Cuvée, made from grapes sourced only from their own vines. It spends more than five years ageing on the lees. Both this and their zero-dosage rosé, pure Pinot Meunier, are more gastro wines to be enjoyed with food. Indeed, this view on how well Hambledon wines pair with food is an important focus for them, so in 2022 they open their Winery Restaurant: an exciting venture with their new head chef, Nick Edgar, who worked for ten years at Raymond Blanc's Manoir aux Quat'Saisons.

Hambledon have dug out a veritable mountain of chalk to create their new winery, which will have space to house some two million bottles (not only Hambledon's, they also offer contract winemaking for other vineyards). The restaurant and a new tasting room will be above the cellar, with views across the vineyards. There are also exciting plans afoot to introduce more cuvées in varying styles, as one would expect traditionally from a leading Champagne house across the Channel.

'We seek energy, precision, length, finesse and balance in our assemblages. We work relentlessly at all of these things to improve our wines year by year. We leave no stone unturned. To me, Hambledon Vineyard is a sunflower seed. At the moment we are tiny, and buried underground, invisible. But soon we will grow tall and beautiful, and the world will see us.'
Ian Kellett

FEATURED WINE: **Première Cuvée**. In a splendid bottle, similar in design to that of Krug, this wine is a Chardonnay-led blend, the rest being a balanced combination of Pinot Noir and Meunier. Produced only in limited quantities, the Première Cuvée is richer in style than their Classic Cuvée and reveals lovely white flowers on the nose, followed by racy acidity with the freshness of tangerines.

LOCAL PRODUCE: **Hand-cut pork pie** from Jake's Artisan Foods made in nearby Petersfield is ideal with a bottle of Hambledon for a tramp along the South Downs Way.

Brown Shrimp, Red Apple, Fennel and Burrata Salad

I chose to use red apples to echo the lovely crisp yet sweet notes of red apple in the Hambledon Vineyard Première Cuvée. This is a lovely light salad for summery days in the garden. When blood oranges are not in season, feel free to swap with peeled segments of fresh clementine. Do assemble this salad at the last minute before serving, to prevent the apple and avocado from discolouring.

SERVES TWO

1 large fennel bulb

2 crisp green celery sticks

2 unpeeled red apples (Red Prince or Worcester Pearmain if you can find them), cored and roughly diced

1 generous tbsp sherry vinegar

3 tbsp extra virgin olive oil

1 blood orange, segmented with no skin or pith

2 small ripe avocados, peeled, stoned and cubed (prepare at the last minute)

70g brown shrimps, cooked and peeled

2 burrata cheeses

Handful of shavings of Parmesan cheese (optional)

Remove the hard base from the fennel and slice the rest very finely, ideally using a mandolin (an amazingly useful piece of kitchen kit but do always use the finger guard).

Halve the celery sticks lengthways if necessary then chop finely into small slices.

Put the prepared apples into a bowl of water acidulated with lemon juice until ready to serve.

Make the salad dressing with the vinegar and oil. Lastly, prepare the avocado.

Arrange all the ingredients except the burrata artistically on individual plates. Drizzle with dressing. Place a burrata in the centre of each salad. Serve if desired with some toasted sourdough.

PS When I was playing around with this recipe, I was overcome by a wave of retro craving, and made a 1970s-style Parmesan basket to serve this salad in. It looked very cute albeit very kitsch, but if you'd like to try that out, don't let me stop you. (Cover the base of a small frying pan with LOTS of grated Parmesan, gently heat until all melted into a pancake shape, remove and place over an upturned small bowl and mould into shape. Leave to cool for 1 minute until solid.)

PPS I have sometimes swapped the brown shrimps for cooked prawns. Or even replaced the burrata with shredded smoked chicken for a variant on surf & turf!

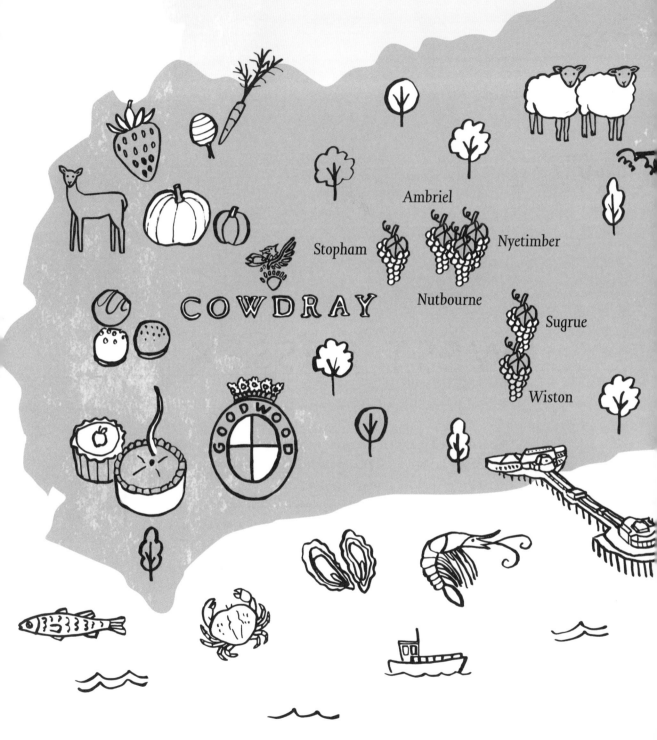

COWDRAY

Stopham

Ambriel

Nyetimber

Nutbourne

Sugrue

Wiston

GOODWOOD

ourne

WEST SUSSEX

Sussex is divided into two counties, with West Sussex nestling up against the border with Hampshire. The South Downs National Park, England's newest national park, covers an area of 628 square miles from Winchester to Eastbourne, encompassing the chalk downs, medieval villages and rolling countryside of Hampshire, West Sussex and East Sussex.

Chichester, famous for its cathedral with a stained-glass window by Marc Chagall, lies on a beautiful natural harbour, an SSSI that is home to seals, curlews and redshanks; picturesque Bosham, whose main street entirely floods twice a day with the tides; the noble estate of Goodwood, with its racecourse, annual hill climb event, Vintage Revival and Festival of Speed; the historic market town of Midhurst, with the Cowdry Ruins dating from Tudor times; the Cowdry estate, famous for world-class polo matches and village houses with buttercup yellow window frames; Arundel with its imposing castle and Sussex Gin Truffles from master chocolatiers, Noble & Stace.

STOPHAM VINEYARD

One of the exciting things about English wines is the freedom enjoyed by winemakers and vineyard owners by not being beholden to centuries of winemaking tradition. For that reason, many of the people featured in this book have come into wine via some unusual careers, bringing with them a huge enthusiasm for English wine. One such is Simon Woodhead, head winemaker at Stopham Vineyard within the South Downs National Park. Simon used to be a designer at TAG McLaren F1, before succumbing to the wine bug, which led him to retraining at Plumpton College in East Sussex.

Their strapline is 'English Wine Made with Precision & Passion in Sussex' and this is aptly reflected in their wines. The vines were planted in 2007 and tended with a sustainable attitude to balance the biodiversity of this beautiful part of West Sussex. A small (but perfectly formed!) winery – with the addition of their pride and joy: a handful of French oak barrels – is where they create multiple award-winning wines. Although they do make a sparkling (served, for example, at the V&A Museum in London), it is for their elegant still whites that they have received endless plaudits from leading wine journalists, including Jancis Robinson, as well as winning the Independent English Wine Awards (IEWA) trophy for best still English wine three years in a row! Stopham still wines are usually my gift of choice when visiting an Italian, Argentinian or French winemaker (add nationalities at will), as the first impressed reaction will always be: *This cannot be English?*

The Stopham single-variety Bacchus is a great benchmark for this flagship white grape, excellent with local Sussex asparagus (possibly with poached egg on top), while their very food-friendly Pinot Blanc is an outstanding version of this white grape – a true delight – with rich melon notes and good structure backed up by balanced acidity. Look out for their newest release: a barrel-fermented Pinot Blanc – almost Burgundian in style. This is exceptionally talented winemaking, resulting in polished yet complex, characterful wines.

'At Stopham, we have the perfect conditions for growing aromatic and sparkling wine varietals. Our 6 hectare vineyard is located within the beautiful South Downs National Park and our south-facing slopes sit on sandy, free-draining soil at a low altitude, maximising our exposure to warmth and sunlight. Our environment means that we have to work sustainably and we pride ourselves on the passion and precision we put into hand nurturing our grapes.'
Simon Woodhead

FEATURED WINE: **Pinot Gris**. In the glass it gives you oodles of ripe tropical fruit and apricots. This slightly off-dry white (please trust me: do not think that it is sweet!) with rich mouthfeel makes it a classic partner for anything with a touch of spice – from braised fennel to roasted saffron potatoes.

LOCAL PRODUCE: **Seven Sisters cheese**, made in Sussex from sheep's milk and coated in seaweed, is perfect with any of the Stopham whites.

Chameleon Curry

Don't panic – not real chameleons! The name of this recipe refers to its inherent flexibility. What started off as a lobster curry morphed into butternut squash curry and my OH has swapped the main protein for everything from prawns to paneer. It is very forgiving; a great Monday evening speedy supper if you have some leftover roast chicken or squash. I am a self-confessed wuss when it comes to chilli, so for those who like a bit of heat, add two thinly sliced red chillies after the desiccated coconut.

The fragrance of the Pinot Gris is the ideal combination with the sweetness of lobster and the warming spices.

SERVES FOUR

Vegetable oil
2 white onions, finely chopped
8 garlic cloves, grated or crushed
4cm piece of fresh ginger, peeled and grated
1 tsp each of ground ginger, turmeric, cumin,
    cinnamon and smoked paprika
Salt flakes
400ml can of coconut milk
200g fresh cherry tomatoes, chopped
50g unsweetened desiccated coconut
Juice of 1 lemon
4 cooked lobster tails (frozen but fully defrosted is
    fine), cut into 2cm cubes
Handful of fresh coriander leaves (optional)
Sea salt and black pepper

Heat two glugs of vegetable oil in a heavy-based saucepan. Add the onions and cook over a low heat for 10–15 minutes until they start to colour, stirring every so often.

Add the garlic and continue cooking for 4 minutes. Add the fresh ginger, spices and about 2 teaspoons of salt flakes. Cook for a couple of minutes, stirring all the time, until the spices start to release their aromas.

Pour in the coconut milk and tomatoes (including any juices). Bring to the boil then reduce the heat and simmer for about 10–15 minutes. The sauce should have thickened slightly.

In a small frying pan (pixie pans are great for this) dry-fry the desiccated coconut until golden. Add to the curry and stir for another 3–4 minutes until it thickens.

Add salt and pepper and lemon juice to taste. You can freeze the sauce at this stage.

Drop the cooked lobster tails into the sauce and warm through completely.

Serve with basmati rice or flatbreads. Fresh coriander, for those who like it, can be sprinkled on at the end.

WISTON ESTATE

The Wiston Estate has been stewarded by the Goring family since 1743, but it was not until 2006 that South African-born Pip Goring and her English husband Harry converted just under 6.5 hectares of their 2,500 hectares of farmland to vines. Pip grew up in the beautiful wine region of Franschhoek, but it was 34 years after she arrived in her new Sussex home before she convinced Harry that the chalk composition of their estate in the rolling South Downs would be ideal for sparkling wines. From the first harvest, the success of the Wiston wines has more than justified Pip's belief.

A key decision from the start was getting winemaker Dermot Sugrue on board. Dermot's deep understanding of their terroir is evident across the range. From the 2022 vintage, the head winemaker will be Marcus Rayner, who has been working alongside Dermot for several harvests. The Goring family believes in minimal intervention in the vineyards; Pip and Harry's eldest son Richard has taken on the running of the estate since 2011 and hosts an environmental charity to protect the Sussex landscape. This philosophy is carried through in the cellars using a large Coquard hydraulic press, for instance, which gives a noticeably light pressing of the grapes and means the Wiston wines are hallmarked by a vibrant yet elegant style.

As well as a passion for wine, the Goring family's love of great food has resulted in their winery restaurant, aptly named Chalk, which focuses on local Sussex produce, such as Sister Sarah Cheese, a semi-soft goat's cheese coated with annatto, giving this bright white cheese a lovely contrasting orange rind.

Wiston produces seven different cuvées of sparkling wine, from the Brut NV to the Blanc de Noirs Vintage, which is blissful with scrambled eggs and local Sussex black truffle as an indulgent brunch.

'I love Wiston's uniqueness and position. It is a dream come true and the story continues.'
Pip Goring

FEATURED WINE: **Sparkling Rosé NV**. A blend of the three classic *champenoise* varieties, with Pinot Noir slightly more dominant over Chardonnay and Pinot Meunier. Although this is a wine ideal at any time of year (or time of day!), its aroma conjures up a hot English summer evening. It has an abundance of red fruit (imagine a basket of raspberries, strawberries, redcurrants and more), followed by crisp minerality. It works well as a simple aperitif, with crispy duck pancakes, salmon mousse or with a delicate dessert, such as the roulade overleaf.

LOCAL PRODUCE: The rich oiliness of **Springs Smokery oak-smoked mackerel** is cut through beautifully by both the Vintage and Non-Vintage sparkling rosés.

Hazelnut Roulade with Rosewater and Raspberries

If you are reading this recipe on a dark, grizzly November day, I urge you to make this roulade and open a bottle of Wiston Sparkling Rosé. You will instantly be transported to a long, lazy, summer Sunday lunch in a sunny English garden. Roulades are a bit of a go-to in my kitchen if I need something that looks very impressive but is a doddle to make, be it sweet or savoury. Although I have suggested raspberries here, you could use redcurrants, rhubarb or strawberries, all of which match the red-fruit aromas in this delectable sparkling wine. As an aside, this rosé is also the ideal wine to serve with sweet-cured bacon and ricotta pancakes for brunch!

SERVES SIX TO EIGHT

4 egg whites

225g caster sugar

50g roasted hazelnuts, finely chopped, plus extra
    to serve

300ml double cream

Rosewater, to taste

200g raspberries, plus extra to serve

Neutral vegetable oil, to grease

Preheat the oven to 180°C fan/200°C/gas mark 6. Grease a Swiss roll tin (23 × 33cm) with neutral vegetable oil and line with baking parchment.

Put the egg whites into the scrupulously clean bowl of a stand mixer. Whisk until stiff points form.

Still whisking, gradually add the sugar, about a heaped teaspoon at a time, and whisk well. By the time all the sugar is added the meringue should be glossy with very stiff peaks. Spread into the prepared tin, sprinkle with the nuts and bake for 8 minutes – it should be lightly coloured.

Reduce the temperature to 140°C fan/160°C/gas mark 3 and bake for another 20 minutes. Meanwhile, lay a large sheet of baking paper on a flat surface.

Remove the meringue from the oven and turn it over onto the sheet of baking paper (the nutty side will be underneath). Carefully peel off the lining paper from the meringue. Allow to cool for about 10–15 minutes.

Meanwhile, whip the cream until soft peaks form. Add the rosewater according to taste. It is quite enthusiastic in flavour, so start with ½ teaspoon and taste to see if you need more.

Spread the whipped cream over the cold meringue and scatter with the raspberries.

Now form it into a Swiss roll shape. Using the base sheet of paper as an aid, roll the meringue firmly from one long side. Wrap in a fresh sheet of baking paper and chill in the fridge for an hour before serving.

Serve the roulade in thick slices, perhaps with more fresh raspberries on the side and a few chopped hazelnuts.

NUTBOURNE

Although part of the Nutbourne estate had been under vines since 1980, it took on its current guise when Peter and Bridget Gladwin were looking for a new home in the countryside with lots of land for their young family of three boisterous boys. They found the perfect manor house, which just happened to come with its own vineyard attached. What followed became a true love affair between the Gladwin family and this charming part of West Sussex.

Nutbourne has 10.5 hectares of vineyards on greensand soils, planted with eight varieties: Chardonnay, Pinots Noir, Blanc, Gris and Meunier, Bacchus, Huxelrebe and Reichensteiner, and their wines are produced exclusively from their own grapes. The still range includes Bacchus, Pinot Noir and Chardonnay and their unique Sussex Reserve, in an attractive flute bottle. The sparkling wines – amusingly all labelled Nutty – are Pinot Noir Blush, the Non-Vintage Wild and the award-winning classic method Vintage Brut, which is a blend of Chardonnay and Pinot Noir.

Alongside their hands-on involvement in the vineyards, Peter is a respected chef with a renowned catering company in London that cooks for many City events such as the Lord Mayor's Banquet, while Bridget is an artist. Her evocative paintings, inspired by the natural beauty of the estate, feature on their wine labels. Their three sons Oliver, Richard and Gregory – chef, restaurateur and farmer respectively – run four London restaurants that showcase the produce of West Sussex, foraging the estate whenever they are home. The family farm rears heritage breeds of cattle, pigs and sheep, so Nutbourne truly has all the elements for the perfect meal.

'We have been privileged to be a part of the English wine scene for over thirty years, watching it grow from an eccentric hobby to the flourishing New World region it is today. Our enthusiasm has never diminished; we aim to inspire every visitor to Nutbourne with the exciting developments of the whole industry.'
Peter Gladwin

FEATURED WINE: **Sussex Reserve**. This distinctive field-blend wine really captures the essence of the Sussex countryside with its Bacchus-driven elderflower bouquet, ample hedgerow fruits and aromatic herbaceous finish. Its dry style makes it ideal as an aperitif or to complement a variety of spicy or fruit-based dishes.

LOCAL PRODUCE: Charlie's Trout **smoked trout pâté** produced in the nearby village of Pulborough is excellent with the estate's Bacchus. **Nutbourne heritage tomatoes**, grown by their neighbours at Nutbourne Nursery, are sold across the south of England and are perfect with a glass of Nutbourne Blush, enjoyed on a picnic rug overlooking the vineyards, which Nutbourne offers during the summer months!

Summer Pudding with Clotted Cream

'I was invited by Cindy-Marie to provide one of my own recipes to complement our Nutbourne Sussex Reserve. Quintessentially English – there is nothing quite like a proper homemade summer pudding to capture the taste and magic of the countryside on a fine summer's day. Although our Sussex Reserve is a dry wine, it is a perfect complement to this classic dessert.' **Peter Gladwin**

SERVES SIX TO EIGHT

1kg fresh summer berries (strawberries, raspberries, blackberries, redcurrants or blackcurrants)
800g frozen berries (to create good juice)
150g caster sugar
100ml water
25ml elderflower cordial
1 slightly stale loaf of medium-sliced white bread, crusts removed
250g clotted cream

You will need a 1.75-litre bowl

Save a few choice fresh berries to decorate the pudding and cut the larger fruit into pieces. Mix these with the frozen berries, sugar, water and elderflower cordial in a heavy-bottomed pan over a low heat. Bring to the boil and simmer for 8–10 minutes. Pour the mixture into a sieve set over a shallow dish to retain the cooked fruits and all the juice. Leave to cool slightly.

Dip a slice of bread into the berry juice and lay it over the base of the serving bowl, juice-side out. Dip four more slices into the juice and place them up the sides of the bowl. Cut and dip triangles of the bread to fill the gaps until all the sides are covered in the juicy bread.

Half-fill the bowl with fruit and top it with a layer of bread. Press down to compact the fruit. Now fill the bowl right up to the brim with fruit and top it with another layer of juice-dipped bread.

Place a small plate on top, press down again and then place a heavy weight on top (a tin of beans will do). Set the bowl on a dish to capture any leakage and leave it in a cool place for 24 hours to set.

Liquidise the remaining fruit and juice and then pass it through a fine sieve. Add a little sugar to taste.

Turn out the pudding, coat it with the liquidised juice and decorate with the reserved fresh berries. Serve with clotted cream.

NYETIMBER

For many Brits, and indeed for many wine lovers and wine writers across the globe, Nyetimber was perhaps the first estate that made them sit up and take note of English sparkling wine. Planted in the 1980s by an American couple who had one sole aim: to make world-class sparkling wine on their West Sussex property. Unusually for that time, when English wine was still almost a cottage industry, they opted to plant only *champenoise* varieties: the Holy Trinity of Chardonnay, Pinot Noir and Pinot Meunier. Fast forward to the mid-1990s, by which time they had notched up an array of awards, and Nyetimber had the world's wine press enthralled. For anyone who still thought that English wine was just a gentle joke, it was a real eye-opener.

The estate sold to its current owner, Eric Heerema, in 2006, and, since 2007, Canadian winemakers Cherie Spriggs and husband Brad Greatrix have overseen the wine production. In 2018, Cherie won the coveted International Sparkling Winemaker of the Year: the first time the award was made to anyone other than a winemaker in Champagne. There has been much investment at Nyetimber and although the original vineyard and its new state-of-the-art winery are in West Sussex, they have expanded the estate to include extensive vineyard plots across Hampshire and Kent. This extended range gives their winemakers a greater variety of grapes and extra volume as well as offsetting the risk of frost affecting the crop of any one region. Despite the huge expansion projects, Cherie and Brad have maintained the quality that set Nyetimber apart in the 1990s, exemplified in their Classic Cuvée, Tillington Single Vineyard, as well as delicious Blanc de Blancs.

'The story of Nyetimber is one of pioneering spirit and passion, with a singular desire to produce wines worthy of the most joyous celebrations.'
Cherie Spriggs

FEATURED WINE: **Cuvee Chérie**. Most wines from the Nyetimber stable have a pure steely acidity whereas this addition of a Demi-Sec gives a wider scope for food and wine pairing. Made solely from Chardonnay with a perfectly judged amount of residual sugar, this gloriously rounded wine happily pairs with desserts (heavenly with Eton Mess) as well as Roquefort or other blue cheese and is well worth trying with chicken liver pâté or lightly spicy foods, such as Pad Thai.

LOCAL PRODUCE: **Lord London cheese** from Alsop & Walker is an unusually shaped cow's milk cheese that has a delicate citrus tang, which works so well with the pure Chardonnay of Nyetimber Blanc des Blancs.

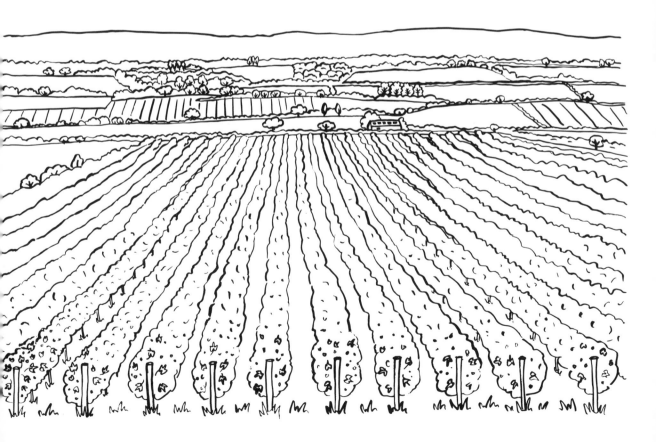

Rhubarb and Custard Afternoon Tea Traybake

The citrus fruit notes of Cuvee Chérie are sublime with the tart rhubarb and comforting custard of this recipe. It may seem a tad retro or simply odd to use custard powder as well as custard in this recipe, but the powder gives a depth of creaminess to the cake.

SERVES TEN

400g rhubarb, trimmed and cut into 2cm pieces
225g caster sugar
Zest and juice of 1 clementine
3 tsp maple syrup
250g butter, softened, plus extra for greasing
3 large free-range eggs
175g self-raising flour
50g custard powder
100g ground almonds
500g tub vanilla custard
50g demerara sugar

Preheat the oven to 210°C fan/230°C/gas mark 8 and line a baking sheet with baking parchment. Grease and line a 28 × 22cm shallow baking tin with parchment too.

Place the rhubarb in a single layer on the baking sheet. Sprinkle with 25g of the caster sugar, the clementine zest and juice and drizzle with maple syrup. Bake for about 25 minutes. Remove from the oven and leave to cool.

Reduce the oven temperature to 180°C fan/200°C/gas mark 6.

In a stand mixer, beat together the remaining caster sugar with the butter, eggs, flour, custard powder, ground almonds and 100g of the custard until pale and creamy. Fold the cooled rhubarb through the batter.

Pour into the lined tin and spread in an even layer. Press deep holes into the mixture with the back of a dessertspoon and pour the remaining custard into the holes.

Bake for about 45 minutes until risen. The sponge should be set but the puddles of custard will still be slightly wobbly.

Sprinkle over the demerara sugar and leave to cool slightly before serving.

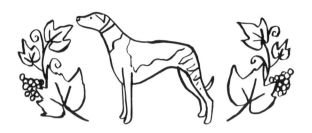

SUGRUE SOUTH DOWNS

Acclaimed winemaker – some say maestro of English sparkling wine – Dermot Sugrue earned his vinous stripes at vintages in Champagne, Pomerol and with the Barton family in St Julien. Subsequently, he was drawn back to the world of opportunity that was just getting exciting in the UK. Starting off as winemaker at Nyetimber which, under his watch, put English quality sparkling wines on the world wine map, he decamped just 10 miles down the road to Wiston where, between 2006 and 2022, he was head winemaker.

At the same time, Dermot planted a 1 hectare vineyard of his own at Storrington Priory, which resulted in the 2009 vintage of his signature wine, The Trouble with Dreams, named after the previous year's harvest was devastated by birds. This first vintage, released in 2013, received all-round plaudits. He has since leased Mount Harry vineyard, near Lewes in East Sussex, the fruit from its chalky soils complementing that from the greensands of Storrington. The incredible attention to detail at every stage, including the use of old Burgundian barrels for some of the ageing, mean the Sugrue wines are superbly balanced between linear precision and slow maturation.

Although Dermot has made wines for quite a few other estates in the south of England, it's his own, Sugrue South Downs, that allows his creativity to soar; to create a single Chardonnay-dominant sparkling wine each year that has no boundaries and is allowed to express the characteristics of each vintage. As well as Dreams, Dermot makes Cuvée Dr Brendan O'Regan, named after his great-uncle, a delightful zero dosage labelled #ZODO, and in 2021 they released their Blanc de Blancs 2015, Cuvée Boz, named after Dermot's late brother.

Dermot was recently joined by his fiancé Ana Đogić, who hails from Croatia. She has worked at some impressive cool-climate estates in Germany and Austria, as well as vintages in NZ and even Peru (her life motto: *Wir sind alle ein bisschen Riesling*, or 'We are all a little bit Riesling'). Ana first came to England as winemaker and lecturer at Plumpton College and is now concentrating fully on Sugrue South Downs and continuing her love of viticulture.

FEATURED WINE: **The Trouble with Dreams**. Each vintage of this almost iconic wine will be quite different. The 2017 is the current release, and you can expect some real complexity from its long maturation. (If you ever lay your hands on a bottle, or even a magnum, of the 2010 vintage, do not hesitate). The style combines citrus freshness with the nerviness of a greyhound, and long, long, rich, nutty, almost buttery structure.

LOCAL PRODUCE: **Winslade cheese**, made over the border in Hampshire, is a heavenly pairing with this wine, especially if studded with garlic and thyme and baked in the oven until gooey. Dip into it with either sourdough or roasted baby potatoes.

Mushroom Strudel with Baron Bigod and Thyme

One of the most classic food choices to pair with aged sparkling vintage wines is mushrooms: they echo the bosky notes that can develop in bottle with age. Although I have specified chestnut mushrooms, you can use a mixture of flavoursome fungi such as shiitake or morels.

Baron Bigod is a glorious unpasteurised brie-style cheese made in Suffolk with milk from Montbéliarde cows (echoes of The Archers!). The rich milk gives an intense creaminess, which also develops a mushroomy character as it ages. As for the pastry, apologies to *The Great British Bake Off*, but life really is too short to make your own filo pastry.

SERVES THREE TO FOUR

270g pack filo pastry sheets
Neutral vegetable oil, for frying
60g unsalted butter, melted, plus a knob for frying
300g chestnut mushrooms, sliced
2 banana shallots, finely chopped
1 large garlic clove, finely chopped
8 thyme sprigs, leaves picked
Splash of English sparkling wine (about 3 tbsp)
25g chives, finely chopped
200g Baron Bigod cheese, diced
30g Parmesan or Old Winchester cheese, grated

Remove the pastry from the fridge about 20 minutes before you start but leave it in the packet: filo pastry dries out quicker than a puddle in the Atacama Desert.

Heat a glug of vegetable oil and a knob of butter in a large frying pan. Add the mushrooms and cook over a high heat for 5 minutes, stirring every minute or so.

When they are soft and browning, add the shallots, garlic and thyme. Add the wine and stir over a high heat until the alcohol has evaporated. Stir in the chives then set aside to cool completely.

Preheat the oven to 200°C fan/220°C/gas mark 7 and lightly oil a large baking sheet.

You are going to make one large strudel parcel so first lay one filo sheet on the baking tray and brush generously with melted butter. Repeat with the rest, layering one on top of the other. (Cover the remaining filo with a clean, damp tea towel as you work to avoid it drying out.)

Spread half the cold filling onto the filo, leaving a 3cm border on all sides. Scatter diced cheese down the centre then cover with rest of the mushroom filling.

To make your strudel parcel, first fold the short ends in, then roll the filo until the filling is sealed (there are handy 'how to' strudel videos online if this worries you). Position the seam underneath. Lightly brush with the remaining melted butter and scatter with the grated cheese.

Bake for 20–25 minutes until crisp and golden. Serve in thick slices, possibly with some creamed celeriac.

Tip – If you want to up the ante on the mushroom flavour, you could brush some porcini mushroom paste on the filo pastry under the mushroom filling or dust on some porcini powder. Or maybe, for a real flavour bomb, stir a spoonful of truffle paste into the mushroom mix.

AMBRIEL

'Ebulliently English' is the apt marketing strapline of the delightful family-run estate of Ambriel near Pulborough. It is owned by Charles and Wendy Outhwaite, following careers as a banker and a barrister respectively. As Wendy says, the couple enjoyed a long-term apprenticeship training their palates by simply drinking lots of different styles of wine before their fascination with the subject led them to plant vineyards in the South Downs in 2008. They have nine hectares of south-facing vines planted on greensand, a wonderfully free-draining bedrock, which is helpful in the marginal – and sometimes damp! – English climate.

As well as being intent on producing delicious wines, they also focus strongly on sustainability in all areas of their production – from practising intelligent viticulture, avoiding monoculture planting in their vineyards by including bee-friendly plants such as dandelions, lavender and thyme to encourage biodiversity, to using vegetable inks on the foil capsules on their bottles. In winter their vineyards are grazed by Ouessant sheep – a rare heritage breed from Brittany and the smallest in the world – and the estate's hedgerows, which attract a wide variety of bird life, are browsed by Golden Guernsey goats.

In a true bid for no waste, Charles also makes fabulous sourdough loaves using the yeast from the vineyard's Chardonnay grape skins.

As well as their Classic Cuvée, award-winning Sparkling Rosé and a Blanc de Noirs, do look out for their flagship wine – Cloud Ten. This Chardonnay-dominant sparkling, which, after an extensive nine years ageing on the lees, is only bottled in magnums – the ideal size for celebration.

'As owners, we're not hands off. Rather we're hands on, and usually hands in. Our toast at Ambriel is "May your wine – like your wit – be Sparkling".'
Wendy and Charles Outhwaite

FEATURED WINE: **English Reserve**. Currently, there are very few demi-sec wines produced in England, and Ambriel's single-vineyard version is truly delightful. Thanks to the higher dosage in the wine, it has a wonderful balance and rounded mouthfeel that means it marries happily not only with desserts (heavenly with lemon meringue pie) but also cheese, such as Blue Clouds, a blue cheese from the nearby Balcombe Dairy, which is similar to a Gorgonzola dolce in style.

LOCAL PRODUCE: Look out for **Burwash Rose** cheese, made in East Sussex, a wonderful semi-soft yet pungent unpasteurised cheese that is washed in English rose water. The floral notes of the cheese work so well with the red fruits of the Ambriel Rosé.

Strawberry and Amaretti Ice Cream Kisses

When I lived in Northern Italy, in the beautiful region of Piemonte, before visiting friends for afternoon tea, I would call into our local *pasticceria*, where exquisite mini cakes perfect for one delicious mouthful — mostly the totally irresistible *Bignole (Bigné) Piemontese*, tiny choux buns stuffed with *crema pasticcera* and gleaming with icing every shade of an artist's palette — were lined up in rows awaiting to tempt before being stylishly packaged.

Sometimes, there would also be another classic, *Baci di Dama*: small, utterly irresistible hazelnut biscuits stuffed with dark chocolate. I started making these for Christmas parties, to serve at the end as a gentle reminder that it was time to go home (friends I do love you all, but you know who the guilty ones are!)

But one hot summer's day, I played around with the idea of a summer version, using almonds instead of hazelnuts and strawberry instead of chocolate. Whilst I am loath to call them *Baci di Dama* and risk incurring the wrath of every Piemontese friend, the Italian delicacies were indeed the inspiration for this delicious recipe.

Well, I call it a recipe — it's more an assemblage, ideal for hot days when minimum time in the kitchen is called for. If you've more time on your hands, you could make your own amaretti and ice cream — but this is for those days when time in the garden, with a chilled glass of Ambriel Sparkling in hand, takes priority.

Ambriel's English Reserve is an explosion of summer fruits in the glass, so perfectly echoed by both the strawberries and raspberries in this recipe — and the sweet almond biscuit balances the autolytic notes of this glorious Demi Sec.

MAKES – AS MANY AS YOU CAN WITHOUT THEM MELTING BETWEEN ASSEMBLAGE AND EATING! SUGGEST MAKING THEM IN SMALL AMOUNTS – AND THEN GO BACK FOR SECONDS!

One tub of good-quality strawberry ice cream (about 500g with leftovers), such as from the Sussex Ice Cream Company

One pack of amarettini (mini amaretti biscuits – the Arden & Amici brand is 100g)
Freeze-dried raspberries (in small pieces or powder – try online from Sous Chef), at least 50g

Get the sparkling and glasses ready, and rope in a friend to be sommelier as these biscuits are to be enjoyed as soon as they're made!

Prepare the ingredients in an assembly line.

Place a small teaspoon of ice cream onto an amarettini biscuit and top with a second biscuit to make a sandwich. Squish slightly so the ice cream reaches to the edges. Roll the edges of the sandwich in the freeze-dried raspberries.

Head to the sunshine and enjoy!

NB – if it's a really hot day you can pop them in the freezer on a baking tray for 10 minutes to firm up. But not too long or the biscuit will lose its crunch! You can also make these using regular-sized amaretti, but napkins will definitely be needed.

ALBOURNE ESTATE

Eight miles inland from the Sussex coast north of the city of Brighton lies the boutique estate of Albourne. Established in 2010 on a low ridge of sandstone in plain sight of the South Downs National Park, Albourne is the realisation of the dream of its owners Alison Nightingale and Nick Cooper after visiting vineyards in Australia and New Zealand. Another alumnus of Plumpton College, Alison is keen on promoting the biodiversity of the estate and reliance on green energy, which is why the roof of the winery buildings supports 129 solar panels. A walk through the peaceful south-facing vineyards, past beehives to a carp-laden lake, gives a real understanding of the focus on sustainability here. Sheep graze in the vineyards during winter months, adding manure to the soil and controlling the ground cover, while trimmed vine prunings mulch the alleyways between the vines.

Albourne wines are made entirely from their own grapes by consultant winemaker Salvatore Leone. Varieties include the classic champagne trio as well as Pinots Blanc and Gris, Bacchus, Ortega and Dornfelder. Their range includes classic sparkling wines, a slightly quirky Bacchus frizzante and a still white Pinot Noir. Look out too for their Pinot Noir, a delicate interpretation of this fickle red variety. They also use their base wines to make a vermouth with a variety of spicy citrusy botanicals – excellent before dinner served simply over ice, or maybe accompanied by a platter of British charcuterie or even as a digestif!

The beautiful backdrop of this Sussex estate is also celebrated on the wine labels, which feature its wildlife visitors in the paintings of local artist Louise Body.

FEATURED WINE: **Estate Selection**. This appealing white wine is made from the top selections of each variety to make a truly delightful blend which varies with each vintage: the current release is Chardonnay, Ortega and Bacchus to give it a multi-layered complexity. Scented hedgerow on the nose leads to zesty lime and elderflower: wonderfully reviving and fresh. Also perfect with seafood.

LOCAL PRODUCE: Try the oak-smoked **Ashdown Forester Cheese** from the High Weald Dairy with Albourne's award-winning still white, the Chardonnay-led Sandstone Ridge.

Roasted Cauliflower, Aubergine and Chickpeas with Tahini Dressing

SERVES TWO (PLUS LEFTOVERS FOR ANOTHER SALAD THE FOLLOWING DAY)

1 large cauliflower, broken into small florets (include the small tender leaves too)

1 tsp (roughly) each of ground turmeric, ground cumin, black mustard seeds, sumac and smoked paprika

Zest and juice of 1½ large lemons (use the remaining half for squeezing over the finished dish)

Olive oil, for marinating

700g jar of chickpeas (Perelló is a good brand), rinsed well, drained and tipped into a bowl

1 aubergine, roughly chopped into 3–4cm squares

2 tbsp tahini (stir it in the jar until smooth beforehand)

Greek yogurt, to taste

Flat-leaf parsley or mint leaves, chopped, to serve

While writing this book, I underwent a culinary Damascene conversion. All my life, I have never quite understood the appeal of chickpeas – those knobbly little nuggets that everyone else raved about. I like hummus but not the unadorned, unmushed real thing. But with time on my hands, the secret was revealed: removing the flaky outer skins of the chickpeas was an absolute gamechanger.

Despite many helpful tips on the internet for how to skin chickpeas quickly by using bicarbonate of soda or putting them in the microwave, I actually enjoy the therapeutic repetitiveness of skinning them by hand. Food is such a sensual thing; it is as much about texture as flavour and aroma.

If you can remember to soak dried pulses the night before, then do check out Red Fox Carlin Peas from Hodmedods, which are British-grown legumes with a similar flavour profile to chickpeas.

This dish is lovely as a stand-alone, but also works with crumbled feta, baked salmon, smoked chicken and more. The white grape varieties in the Albourne Estate Selection blend vary from vintage to vintage but the Chardonnay, Ortega and Bacchus pick up on many of its flavours – the nuttiness of chickpeas, the vibrant warmth of the spices…

Two hours before cooking, put the cauliflower florets into a large ceramic bowl, sprinkle with the ground turmeric, cumin, mustard seeds and the juice of 1 lemon and coat with a generous amount of olive oil. Stir, cover with a clean tea towel, and leave to marinate at room temperature. Give it a stir every 20 minutes or each time you pass by on the way to the kettle.

Find a comfy chair and sit with the bowl of drained chickpeas, plus a spare bowl for the skins, at table height, otherwise your arms will ache after a while. The task of skinning the chickpeas is best done while listening to an audiobook or some background music! Rub each chickpea to remove the skins and put the skinned chickpeas into the second bowl. Discard the skins.

Preheat the oven to 180°C fan/200°C/gas mark 6. Select a large baking tray or roasting dish, scatter in the cauliflower, aubergine and chickpeas and mix well together. Sprinkle with the sumac and smoked paprika and drizzle with olive oil. Roast for 12 minutes, then remove from the oven and toss the veg, to turn them onto the other side. Return to the oven and cook for a further 15 minutes or until the cauliflower and aubergine pieces are coloured and slightly charred.

Meanwhile, put the tahini in a small bowl, add the juice of ½ lemon and enough olive oil and yogurt to make a dressing. Taste and season with salt if necessary.

Serve in warmed shallow bowls, drizzled with dressing and sprinkled with lots of chopped herbs.

Davenport

Ridgeview

Plumpton

Hoffma
& Rathb

Henners

PEA THROWING

Rathfinny

BRIGHTON PIER

EAST SUSSEX

East Sussex extends along the south coast, from the pebble beaches of Brighton to the cobbled streets of Rye and inland over the High Weald, an Area of Outstanding Natural Beauty, to the borders with Surrey and Kent.

The county town of Lewes, known for the bonfire societies that parade through it on 5 November before gathering at their respective bonfires, for its tiny twittens (a local name for narrow alleyways) and Norman castle, is host to the World Pea Throwing Championship. The city of Brighton and Hove boasts exotic architecture, with the Royal Pavilion, built as a pleasure palace for George IV, and a 1,722-foot long Victorian pier. Brighton is also the eco-capital of England, home to Silo, the first zero-waste restaurant in Britain. A little-known culinary fact is that a modern classic British dessert, banoffee pie, was created in East Sussex in 1971.

Beautiful sand dunes await at Camber Sands; the medieval town of Rye hosts the famous Scallop Festival; the white sea cliffs, the Seven Sisters, are a famous reminder that this is chalk country; beers from the inventive team of brewers and blenders at Burning Sky brewery, tucked away in a South Downs village; and family-run (now seventh-generation) Harvey's (sadly no relation) using four local hops for their Best Bitter brewed in Lewes.

RIDGEVIEW

Ridgeview is another venture that is very much a family affair, the dream of Mike and Chris Roberts, who planted the three traditional champagne grape varieties at their estate in Ditchling, East Sussex, in 1995, way before this was the norm in England. A pioneer of quality English sparkling wine, Mike not only created one of its leading producers, as chairman of the English Wine Producers, he dedicated much of his time to helping to advance, protect and promote the wider industry: a truly inspirational character.

Ridgeview is now run by the Roberts' daughter, Tamara, CEO, and son, Simon, Director of Winemaking, along with their respective other halves. Walking through the bluebell wood down to their vineyards or standing in their tasting room with spectacular views across the South Downs, Ridgeview has an indefinable sense of place. This is backed up by a strong family work ethic, along with endless enthusiasm and energy. Their commitment to quality is reflected in the large presence of Ridgeview sparkling wines in key export markets – no small feat. But their award in 2010 from *Decanter Magazine* of 'Best Sparkling Wine in the World' for their 2006 Blanc de Blancs opened a few doors in wine-loving countries including the United States, Japan and Scandinavian nations. The following year, their exquisite Cuvée Merret Fitzrovia Rosé was served at Her Majesty the Queen's state banquet at Buckingham Palace to welcome President Barack Obama.

Their pristine cellar, with the juxtaposition of shiny stainless steel and immaculate oak barrels, was one of the first in England to have an underground ageing cellar. Currently, Ridgeview have seven sparkling wines: three in their classic Signature range; another three more complex ones in their Limited Release range; while their seventh, Oak Reserve, first released in 2020, is an enticing barrel-fermented Chardonnay, of which only 2,600 bottles were made.

'Celebration is at the heart of Ridgeview and we delight in being part of the moments that matter in people's lives, whether that is with us here, at their favourite restaurant or at home with their friends and family.'
Tamara Roberts

FEATURED WINE: **Blanc de Noirs**. One of their Limited Release range, this award-winning wine is a revelation in a glass. Bursting with freshness, lots of red apples and cherries on the nose, yet at the same time the wonderful toasty brioche notes more often associated with vintage champagne. A blend of the two red grapes, Pinot Noir and Pinot Meunier, it shows power tempered with great balance of fruit and acidity. If you have the patience (a better person than I am!), do give it a bit of time in the glass, as it really develops and opens up. Excellent with oily fish as in the recipe overleaf but also at home with poultry such as quail or poussin.

LOCAL PRODUCE: Delicate **raspberry macarons**, such as those made locally by Creamroll, are irresistible with the Ridgeview Fiztrovia Rosé.

Mackerel Tacos with Gooseberry Compote

One of the most classic pairings, mackerel with gooseberries, allegedly dates back to the Norman Conquest. The richness of this oily fish is cut through by the bright lively acidity of the Ridgeview sparkling. Although for ease I've gone with shop-bought tacos here, these are delicious with homemade flatbreads too. I love this combo of flavours so much, I have even cooked it as a risotto – again, heavenly with the Ridgeview bubbles.

SERVES TWO

150g gooseberries, topped and tailed
Fresh horseradish root, peeled, to taste
75g salted butter, plus extra for greasing
4 fresh mackerel fillets
25g golden caster sugar
Grating of nutmeg
4 soft corn tacos (or flatbreads)

Tip the gooseberries into a saucepan. Add enough cold water to just cover the fruit and bring to the boil. Simmer until soft and starting to break apart then remove from the heat. Use a stick blender to blitz until smooth.

Preheat the oven to 180°C fan/200°C/ gas mark 6.

Finely grate some fresh horseradish root into the fruit compote – aim for about a tablespoon or according to taste. (Mind your eyes, because grating the fresh root releases its volatile oils, which can be quite potent; you can use hot horseradish from a jar if preferred.)

Lightly butter an ovenproof dish. Lay the fish fillets skin-side down in the dish and dot with the butter. Cover with foil and bake for 15 minutes.

Meanwhile, return the saucepan of compote over low to medium heat, add the sugar and a generous grating of nutmeg. Taste – the fruit should be quite sharp.

Warm the soft tacos, either for 5 minutes max in the oven or 2 minutes on each side in a dry frying pan over medium heat.

Lay the fish fillets on each taco or you can flake the fish if preferred, which also removes the skin. Top with gooseberry compote and roll up. Eat straight away with lots of napkins to hand. Good with a side salad of beetroot.

Tip: you can grill or barbecue the fish rather than bake it to give a smokier dimension that works well. Baking just keeps your house smelling less fishy! For a speedy version for lunch, you could make this with prepacked smoked mackerel fillets from the chilled counter – remove the skins, warm slightly and add a good-quality gooseberry compote.

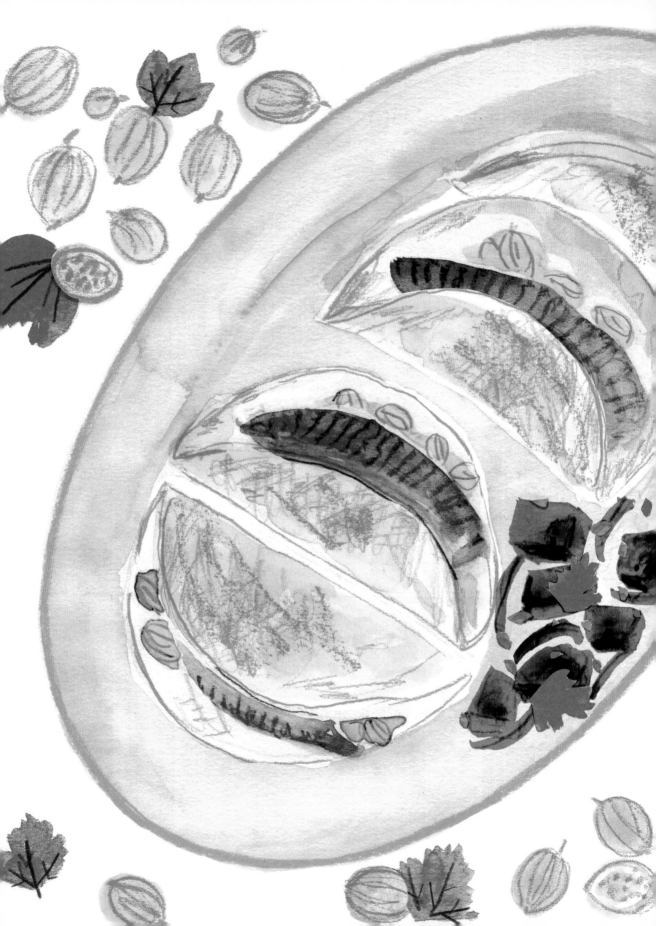

PLUMPTON COLLEGE

As you flick through the producer profiles of this book, one word crops up repeatedly: Plumpton – it could almost appear on each page. The Wine Division of Plumpton College in East Sussex is the only institution in Europe to teach both wine production and the wine business in English. Very few of the current English wine estates have not benefited from Plumpton in some way. The college has trained some of our most exciting viticulturalists (those hardy sorts who look after the vineyards) and winemakers.

Started by the determination of Chris Foss, who was responsible for the creation of the Wine Division in 1988 and who remained its Director until 2019, and now under the excellent aegis of Dr Greg Dunn, Plumpton has given so much to the English wine industry and continues to lead the way in R&D, trialling seemingly any aspect of winemaking from using Georgian-style terracotta amphora to focusing on global warming and disease in the vines.

In addition to academic and business courses up to masters degree level, the college offers vocational apprenticeships. The team in charge of Plumpton's experimental vineyard demonstrates both pruning and trellising techniques, trialling individual grape varieties as well as experimenting with clones of Pinot Noir, collecting temperature data and studying vineyard pests, such as the spotted wing drosophila. But Plumpton also has 10 hectares in nearby Ditchling, which is run as an independent vineyard, making and selling its wines commercially, with the profits fed back into the college's development, and an experimental vineyard at Rock Lodge, near Scaynes Hill. A wide range of varieties is grown to give students in-depth and varied experience. These include Ortega, Rondo and Dornfelder as well as the classic ones such as Chardonnay and Bacchus.

'Making high quality wine is important for the reputation of Plumpton College as an internationally-recognised provider of grape and wine education across all levels. We make a broad range of wine styles at Plumpton in order to expose students to a range of winemaking techniques and issues. Bacchus is one of our key cultivars and is important to the UK wine industry more broadly. Wine and food are in many ways inseparable, so it is exciting to see our single varietal Bacchus paired with food in this excellent publication.'

Dr Greg Dunn

FEATURED WINE: **Bacchus**. What other wine could be chosen for Plumpton than their interpretation of this white grape, fast becoming the flagship variety of English wine. With lovely notes of lime zest, crisp green apples and gooseberry it is absolute zingy freshness personified.

LOCAL PRODUCE: **Sourdough bread** from Flint Owl Bakery in nearby Lewes, topped with Sussex Charmer cheese, makes an awesome cheese on toast.

Asparagus Pappardelle with Salted Ricotta

Perfect for when local asparagus is in season, this light pasta dish combines the tangy greenness of this glorious vegetable with the saltiness of the cheese. Can one taste colours? I think so. The green acidity and zing of Bacchus works so well with asparagus and salted ricotta made at the High Weald Dairy in Sussex. Like most dishes, its enjoyment will depend greatly on the quality of the pasta, so it's worth upgrading, for not many more coins, to a decent brand of dried pasta. Look for one where the label indicates 'bronze die' or *trafilata al bronzo*, meaning the pasta has been made using bronze forms for shaping; this gives each piece a more textured edge for the sauce to cling to, exactly what is wanted for combined deliciousness. Although I have suggested pappardelle, this recipe would be equally happy made with any long wide pasta such as fettuccine or tagliatelle. Salted ricotta is a hard cheese, firm enough to grate, unlike regular ricotta. It is a good one to have in the fridge as well as Parmesan – the two are not totally interchangeable in recipes, but *ricotta salata* adds the same boost of salinity to dishes where you might otherwise use Parmesan or even pancetta.

SERVES TWO (EASY TO DOUBLE UP)

50ml double cream
2 large egg yolks
50g salted ricotta (or to taste), grated
About 25g butter
Olive oil, for frying
150g asparagus tips (use the rest for a soup or tossed through a warm grain salad later)
180g dried pappardelle (Rummo is a good brand)
Handful of chives, snipped with scissors

Mix the cream, egg yolks and roughly two-thirds of the cheese in a bowl.

Bring a large (the largest you have) saucepan of well-salted water to the boil – pasta likes space to swim!

Heat a large frying pan with a knob of butter and a glug of olive oil. Fry the asparagus tips until tender (about 4–5 minutes depending on thickness).

Meanwhile, cook the pasta according to the packet instructions. When al dente, lift the pasta strands from the saucepan with a pair of tongs into the frying pan (do not shake off the water as this is needed to amalgamate the sauce and pasta, which is why tongs work better than draining the pasta into a colander).

Briefly stir once to combine and remove from the heat. Stir in the egg mixture, letting it coat every strand of pasta – add a couple of spoonfuls more of pasta cooking water if required.

Serve immediately in warm pasta bowls: it is important they are warm for this recipe, or the sauce can go claggy very quickly. Sprinkle with rest of the cheese and chopped chives.

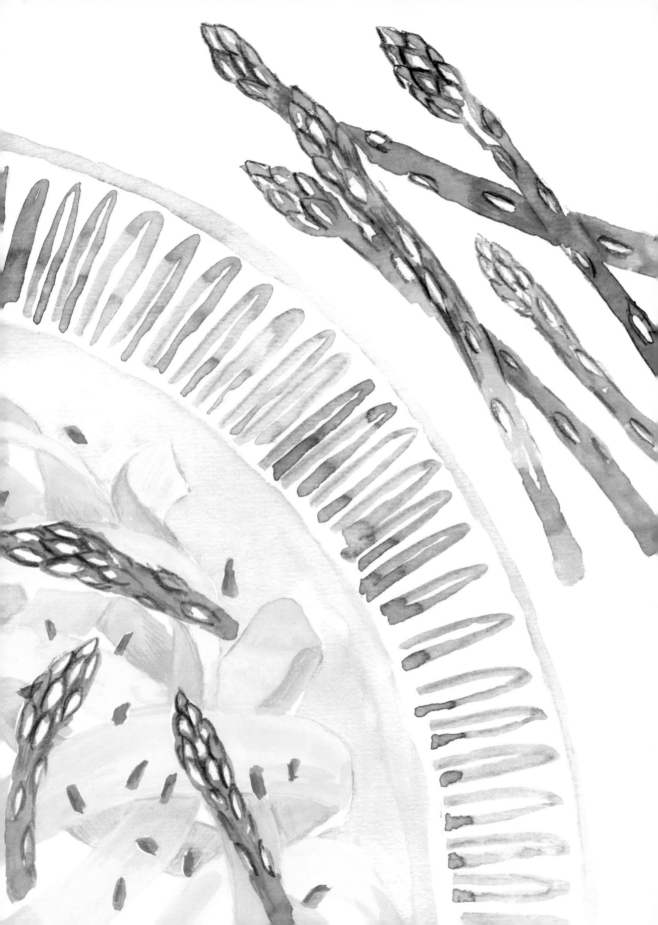

RATHFINNY

Some three miles inland from the East Sussex coastline lie the extensive vineyards of Rathfinny. The estate produces excellent wines but is also a showcase for the future of English wine tourism. At their property overlooking the English Channel, situated inside the winery itself, is an inviting restaurant. Head chef Chris Bailey, formerly at the renowned Black Rat Restaurant in Winchester, creates menus that feature the finest seasonal produce available from the land, sea and garden of the British Isles, all designed to complement the Rathfinny wines. There is also accommodation in beautiful flint barns, so you can stay on the vineyard as well.

Owners Mark and Sarah Driver started this project in 2010 and have been instrumental in gaining recognition for Sussex as a protected denomination for the wines created in the county. Given their plans to export more than 50% of their wines, this may well work very successfully for the competitive overseas markets. Rathfinny produce four sparkling wines, from their signature Blanc de Noirs with the Pinot Noir singing in the glass, through to their Blanc de Blancs, made from the Burgundian clones of rich Chardonnay, as well as their Classic Cuvée and finally their Sparkling Rosé, which is an appealing shade of cerise, made from mostly Pinot Noir, and simply delicious!

They also make some still wines, under the Cradle Valley label, the white featured below, plus a small amount of Hobbs Hawth Red, a blend of Pinots Noir and Précoce and a delicate, pale pink rosé. For a full immersion in Rathfinny, a lunch at their winery restaurant could start with their Dry Vermouth, made from their Pinots Gris and Blanc and end with their Seven Sisters Sussex Brandy, produced from six grape varieties grown on the estate!

'Our ambition is that in twenty years' time you will walk into a bar or restaurant in New York or Beijing and you'll be asked, "Would you like a glass of champagne or a delicious glass of Sussex? I can recommend Rathfinny."'
Mark and Sarah Driver

FEATURED WINE: **Cradle Valley White**. A blend of Pinot Blanc and Pinot Gris (and in some vintages a splash of Chardonnay) shows how these two varieties complement each other. With its nice citrus nose, and a hint of pepper on the finish, this works well as a relaxing summer white with a platter of *fruits de mer*.

LOCAL PRODUCE: **Smoked duck breast** from the Weald Smokery is perfect with Rathfinny's Pinot Noir dominant Sparkling Blanc de Noirs.

Linguine with Crab, Bottarga and Lemon

Such a simple dish I hesitate to call it a recipe but, although simple, it is so full of flavour and matches the aromatic spicy notes of the Pinot Gris in this wine so well, that it screamed out for its inclusion.

Originally hailing from Sicily and Sardinia, bottarga is salted and dried fish roe that can be from grey mullet (caught at sea, so no muddy taste) or tuna. Often seen as a luxurious addition that adds an umami punch to many a dish – a sort of a fishy version of a black truffle – bottarga can be an acquired taste. But it can be particularly useful in the same way anchovies are to impart a deep salty savour to a dish. You can buy it as a whole piece to grate as needed or ready grated in small jars. Purists rightly insist the flavour is better when freshly grated, as it bursts with saline freshness, but I have been known to use a top-quality brand in a jar when bottarga cravings kick in! If you are not a fan, feel free to omit the bottarga from the dish – it will still be delicious.

SERVES FOUR

320g linguine (spaghetti or bucatini will also work)
400g white crab meat
1 garlic clove, grated
Finely grated zest of 1 lemon, and juice of ½
Extra-virgin olive oil, for drizzling
Bottarga, freshly grated (optional)

Bring a large pan of salted water to the boil and cook the pasta according to the pack instructions.

Meanwhile, mix the crab meat, grated garlic and lemon zest together. Season to taste. Make sure the crab meat is well flaked.

Drain the cooked pasta, reserving a tablespoonful of the water, and return to the warm pan off the heat. Toss through a generous amount of extra-virgin olive oil and add the crab mix and lemon juice. Stir well to combine. (If needed, add a spoonful of the cooking water to help emulsify the sauce.)

Serve in warmed pasta bowls and grate some bottarga over the pasta to finish. Bottarga is quite a pungent flavour, so I normally do three flourishes with a fine (microplane) grater before serving and offer guests more to grate at the table once tasted.

DAVENPORT VINEYARDS

Grape growers the world over are at the mercy of the elements and nature: frost, hail, insufficient or too much heat, rot, depredation by birds or insects… there are many things that threaten a good harvest. Added to this, the latitude of the British Isles puts them at the northern limit for successfully growing grapes, so English wine producers are each year subjected to variable, nail-biting-inducing weather; *Vitis vinifera* is, after all, originally a warm-climate species. So, back in 2000, when Davenport's owner and winemaker Will Davenport converted all his vineyards and winery to follow organic principles, a number of people thought he was mad. Instead, he has repeatedly shown that organic grape growing can and does work commercially, even in the humid climate of England. Although the winery is in East Sussex, it is a truly short hop over the county boundary into Kent, to Will's other vineyards at Horsmonden. Davenport Vineyards now have ten hectares of vines in five different locations with nine different grape varieties used to make a selection of dry white, red and sparkling organic wines.

Will studied winemaking at the acclaimed Roseworthy College in Australia, and worked on a wine estate down under as well as working in wineries in California and Alsace. Growing grapes organically brings with it a whole new set of challenges and needs a team that fully understands what is involved – so at Davenport that means everything from hand weeding to increased biodiversity in the vineyards. This non-interventionist attitude is carried through into the Davenport cellar, where there is no fining or use of selected yeasts. Such is the attention to detail, even the final carbon footprint of each bottle – where it is sold – is taken into consideration.

Impressively, in 2014 Davenport won the Gore-Browne trophy for the best UK wine and the only organic winner ever. Also, it is important to give a shout out to the vineyard team at Davenport that won the WineGB Vineyard Pruning Championship – for the second time!

Some of the wines produced are one-off releases according to how the grapes behave in a particular vintage, which makes Davenport an exciting estate to follow. As well as traditionally made sparkling wines, the range includes a Pét Nat (aka Pétillant Naturel, naturally sparkling, so-called 'Hipster Bubbles'!), a Huxelrebe that has had some noble rot (the *good* rot responsible for Sauternes) and a rather delightful, fragrant white blend of Bacchus, Ortega and three other varieties. The first release of their pure Chardonnay sparkling wine was in 2022. This Blanc de Blancs from the 2015 vintage saw long ageing on the lees, which gives tempting notes of baked apples and custard, but with pure clean acidity.

'It's over 30 years since I planted our first vines in 1991, and over 20 years organic certified and I'm still learning! My aim: top quality wine at minimal cost to the environment. It is harder work and needs technical skill, focus, knowledge and experience, but most of all it requires a sense of trust that the wines will achieve their own natural balance to reflect each vintage.

Managing the farm organically is essential for me. I think organic viticulture makes better quality wine and also is better for the planet. I see the benefits every day in our vineyards.'

Will Davenport

FEATURED WINE: **Pinot Noir**. This fickle, capricious variety is seen as the Holy Grail by many winemakers around the world, so the result that Will (and key vineyard manager Phil Harris) have achieved under organic cultivation is super impressive. The 2018 vintage was a gorgeous dark colour with cherries and slight hint of smoke on the finish.

LOCAL PRODUCE: For an easy starter served with the Pinot Noir, do try it with **venison bresaola** from local producer Sussex Gourmand – or their cured meat platter.

Butternut Squash Gnocchi with Amaretti and Sage

225g floury potatoes (unpeeled weight)
250g butternut squash (unpeeled weight)
1 medium egg, beaten
75–100g plain flour
100g salted butter
20 fresh sage leaves
4 amaretti biscuits, crushed
Seaweed salt and black pepper

Combined with my favourite pasta 'sauce' of fried sage and brown butter, the gnocchi here are a hug on a plate. Amaretti might sound an odd addition, but these almond biscuits are traditionally used in Emilia Romagna to stuff fresh pasta and bring a lovely sweetness to an otherwise savoury dish. Although I have made many a variation over the years, this recipe is inspired by the brilliant John Whaite. I have added seaweed salt from the team at Cornish Sea Salt, as I think it brings yet another dimension of umami deliciousness!

The Davenport Pinot Noir delivers a myriad of nuances and has a depth of flavour that sits very happily with the sweetness of the amaretti and savoury earthiness of the sage.

SERVES FOUR AS A STARTER

Peel the vegetables and cut into 2cm chunks. Place into cold salted water, cover with a lid and bring to the boil over a high heat. Turn down to a simmer and cook for 12–15 minutes until the vegetables are tender. Drain well and leave to air dry in a tilted colander (so that air can circulate) for 5–10 minutes.

Once cool, squash the vegetables through a potato ricer into a bowl (or simply mash well in the pan and transfer to a bowl). Add the egg and 50g of the flour and season. Mix until the dough comes together.

Flour a large chopping board with half the remaining flour and separate the dough into four portions. Place one portion on the board and roll into a large sausage shape, around 2cm in diameter. Cut into 2cm pieces and repeat with the rest of the dough. Add more flour if the gnocchi are very sticky, but not too much or the texture can get a bit heavy.

Bring a large pan of salted water to the boil. Place a large shallow casserole or frying pan over a low heat. The trick now is to cook the gnocchi in batches, then add them to the pan of herb butter to cook them until golden on one side, while keeping them warm.

Add the butter to the pan. Once melted, add the sage leaves and fry gently until crisp.

Add about a third of the gnocchi to the boiling water. As soon as they float to the top, scoop them out with a slotted spoon and add to the pan of herb butter. Repeat until all the gnocchi are in the sage butter. Leave for 1–2 minutes – the bases will caramelise in the butter and turn slightly golden.

Serve in warmed shallow dishes, making sure you share out the crispy sage leaves equally, drizzled with any remaining browned butter from the pan. Scatter over the crushed amaretti biscuits and serve!

HENNERS VINEYARD

Standing amid vines on steep, sunny, south-facing slopes next to the Pevensey Levels Nature Reserve, listening to the small team of Henners Vineyard – young but super-knowledgeable and enthusiastic – one could not fail to be excited at all their plans for this gorgeous boutique estate. Hiding away down a leafy narrow country lane, close to Herstmonceux Castle, with the South Downs Way at the boundary of their estate and little more than four miles from the coast, Henners benefits from an ideal microclimate for growing grapes being at low altitude with onshore breezes minimising frost risk and reducing the threat of disease.

The estate was named by its first owner, Lawrence Warr, after one of his French ancestors, Henners Dubois, who fled to England during the French Revolution. Warr, who had previously been a Formula One engineer, set up the 2.8 hectare vineyard in 2007. Fast forward a decade, during which Warr established close ties and a good relationship with Boutinot, his UK agent, and there was a natural synergy for Boutinot to take over the vineyard when Warr offered it for sale.

Currently Henners have planted the classic champagne varieties – Chardonnay, Pinot Noir and Pinot Meunier – but there are multiple clones of each variety, giving a broader palette for flavours to work with. (Plus, watch this space for future experimentation with varieties). From these three grapes they produce four sparkling wines, all secondary bottle-fermented, in their small but well-designed cellars at the vineyard. They produce a couple of still wines, a delicate rosé and an appealing blend of Bacchus and Chardonnay, under the Gardner Street label, which was the historical name of the village of Herstmonceux. The 2014 Chardonnay-dominant Vintage Sparkling is truly outstanding, with beautiful exotic notes of pineapple with tangerine. In their Native Grace range they also make a limited edition multi-vintage Prestige Cuvée and the Chardonnay featured below. All these wines sport stunning labels inspired by the work of Northumbrian-born artist Thomas Bewick (1753–1828), whose enchanting wood engravings of English countryside, wildlife and people, were mentioned by Charlotte Bronte in *Jane Eyre*.

Henners also make a very attractive and rather too easy to drink gin, distilling their own wine in copper stills, using botanicals that bring not only aromas but also texture from the natural oils, giving the gin a wonderful cloudiness when ice is added.

'Boutinot now make wine in the Old World (Cairanne, France), New World (Wildeberg, South Africa), and the "Next World"… England! We really believe that collectively English wine is on the right path and the future of the "next world" is hugely exciting for all of us.'

Eric Monnin, Boutinot Winemaker

FEATURED WINE: **Native Grace Barrel Chardonnay**. This is an example of great winemaking, using a combination of old and new oak barrels that do not smother the fruit but lend it structure. Here is elusive smokiness, the texture of nashi pears and a delightful long finish. This is a lovely example of what still English Chardonnay can be, given the right vintage conditions.

LOCAL PRODUCE: Mangalitsa pigs originate from Hungary and produce fabulous succulent slow-grown pork. In East Sussex, **Beal's Farm** make delicious British charcuterie from the breed, including wonderful air-dried coppa and lomo, which goes so well with Henners Sparkling Rosé.

Roasted Monkfish Tail with 'Nduja, White Beans and Samphire

The original dish that I planned to match with this wine was whole roasted turbot with fennel – and that would be delicious. But after a splendid tasting at Henners, I enjoyed a fabulous barbecued monkfish at the outstanding restaurant The Salt Room in Brighton. The smokiness of the 'nduja balances the barrel ferment, though you can replace it with smoked paprika for a less punchy element in the dish, while the 'meaty' texture of the monkfish is heaven with this wine. I was so taken with enjoying the English wine, the English seafood and great company, I neglected to ask the Chef for the recipe, so this is my reinvention from that inspiration.

SERVES TWO

Large jar of alargada white beans (about 700g
    undrained weight)*
Olive oil, for frying
1 large white onion, finely chopped
115g 'nduja
400–450ml vegetable stock (homemade if possible –
    keep on a simmer until needed)
1 monkfish tail (800g–1kg) – whole on the bone,
    skin and membrane removed
30g butter
100g samphire
Sea salt and black pepper

To serve:
Extra-virgin olive oil
Smoked paprika (optional)
Zest of 1 lemon

* The Perelló brand of alargada white beans is excellent but you can also make this with butter beans or even chickpeas. Do, however, buy them in jars not cans, as the texture and taste is so much better.

Please do read the method first because you can either cook the beans while the fish is cooking, or get ahead and prepare earlier – the beans (before the samphire is added) are very forgiving at being reheated. You won't use all of the beans from a large jar but they are delicious next day as a salad with tomatoes and feta, or even on toast with some bacon!

Empty out the white beans into a sieve, rinse and drain.

Heat a couple of glugs of oil in a large, heavy-based casserole (Le Creuset style) over a medium heat. Add the onions and leave to soften but not colour – about 10 minutes – stirring occasionally. Turn down the heat if they start to catch.

Add the 'nduja and, keeping the heat low, mix in well until it breaks down completely and the onions take on a rich red colour – about 5 minutes.

Tip in the drained beans and mix well with the onions. Add the heated stock and stir well again. Smush a couple of spoonfuls of the beans against the side of the casserole with a cooking spoon. This will give the dish a creamy texture. Continue to cook over a gentle heat for about 15 minutes – keep an eye on the stock level and add bit more if required.

Preheat the oven to 130°C fan/150°C/ gas mark 2.

Season the monkfish lightly with salt (bear in mind the samphire will give lots of saltiness to the dish).

Melt the butter until foaming in a large frying pan. Brown the monkfish on all sides (allow 4–5 minutes) and transfer to a roasting tin. Pour melted butter from the pan over the fish. Place in the preheated oven for 20 minutes, then turn the fish over and cook for further 20 minutes.

Remove from the oven, cover with aluminium foil, and set aside to rest for 10 minutes.

Ensure the bean mixture is hot and stir through the samphire – just enough to warm it through for 1 minute so that it does not lose its crunch. Do not be tempted to add more salt – the samphire will be naturally salty enough.

To serve, portion beans and samphire onto two plates, slice each fillet of monkfish down the side of the bone and place on the beans and samphire, drizzle with extra-virgin olive oil and a pinch of smoked paprika. Finish with fresh lemon zest.

HOFFMANN & RATHBONE

Having spent far too many hours at wine tastings, I truly still love that moment when I taste a wine that makes my at-times jaded palate sing and my eyes spring open in absolute delight. One such moment was on my first encounter (and all subsequent ones) with the wines made with real passion and attention to detail by Hoffmann & Rathbone, a boutique winery in the picturesque village of Mountfield in East Sussex.

The company takes its name from its owners, winemaker Ulrich Hoffmann and Birgit Rathbone. Hailing from Germany, Ulrich had an impressive and varied winemaking career in Germany, Bordeaux, Spain, Napa, Italy and Lebanon before falling in love with the Sussex countryside (and Birgit, now his wife!). Such experience has honed his winemaking skills across a host of climates and grape varieties, which is evident in his skilful handling of the sometimes-searing acidity of grapes grown to make sparkling wine in England's marginal cool climate. This Ulrich achieves by long ageing on the lees, which softens the inherent acidity but still retains freshness. The reward for his patience is sparkling wines that are rich, luscious, complex and truly seductive in the glass.

In the cellars Ulrich ages his wines in a variety of casks – both French and German oak, Spanish chestnut and acacia wood – which brings an extra dimension of complexity to the wines. He also uses shaped terracotta vessels, which means the wine on the lees stays in constant motion, preventing the yeast from resting or settling, allowing the maximum flavours to be achieved in a very gentle way.

Although primarily focusing on sparkling wines, which include their Classic Cuvée, Rosé Réserve, and their truly outstanding Blanc de Blancs, Hoffmann & Rathbone also produce so-called 'special edition' still wines: a very small amount of Bacchus and Pinot Noir. Suitably enough, the 120-year-old yeast used to ferment the single-vineyard Bacchus is known as 'Sleeping Beauty'.

'Nothing is released until it is ready to be sold and unless
it is worthy of the brand.'
Ulrich Hoffmann

FEATURED WINE: **Pinot Noir NV3**. The H&R
Pinot Noir is unusual in that instead of being
a wine from one vintage it is a blend across
three vintages, which allows Ulrich to really
balance the expression of the different years
together. The result is a standout example of
English Pinot Noir: delicious crisp red fruits,
raspberries and a touch of nutmeg on the
palate. The texture of this cool-climate still
wine is impressive in its silkiness.

LOCAL PRODUCE: **Sussex Camembert** from
Alsop & Walker is the ideal match for the
Hoffmann & Rathbone Blanc de Blancs. The
creaminess and bosky notes of the cheese
is the perfect balance with their Vintage
Sparkling Blanc de Blancs with its lovely
rich apple and toasty tones.

Braised Pork Shoulder

Pinot Noir may be a fickle grape variety to grow but it is wonderfully food friendly and matches very well with a surprising range of savoury dishes, from fresh tuna steaks to game. Pork seems to divide people over whether it should be paired with white or red wine – the simple answer is, with what other flavours are you cooking? Here the fennel and the sweetness of the leeks make a handsome duo with the bright fruit notes of this Sussex Pinot Noir.

SERVES SIX

4 tsp fennel seeds

Finely grated zest from 1 large orange

5 fat garlic cloves – 2 whole, 3 crushed

Olive oil, for frying

2kg boned, rolled pork shoulder

3 leeks, finely sliced

175ml dry English white wine

1 tbsp English mustard

2 fennel bulbs, sliced (do use any fragrant feathery fronds)

1 large jar cannellini beans (about 600g drained weight) – El Navarrico is a good brand

350ml chicken stock (homemade if possible)

Cider vinegar, for drizzling

Sea salt and black pepper

The day beforehand, put the fennel seeds, orange zest, the 2 whole garlic cloves and some sea salt and black pepper in a small blender and blitz until fine. Stir in two generous glugs of olive oil. Rub this all

136

over the pork, skin side too. Cover and return to the fridge overnight.

The following day, take the meat out of the fridge an hour before cooking.

Preheat the oven to 210°C fan/230°C/gas mark 8. Heat a small amount of olive oil in a heavy-based, ovenproof (Le Creuset style) casserole and gently cook the leeks and crushed garlic until softened but not coloured.

Add the wine, mustard and fennel. Bring to the boil. Stir in the drained, well-rinsed beans and chicken stock and return to the boil.

Place the marinated meat, skin-side up, on top of the beans, nestling it slightly into the veg and liquid. Drizzle the skin with olive oil and roast for 30 minutes, uncovered.

Reduce the temperature to 140°C fan/160°C/gas mark 2. Remove the casserole, cover with the lid and return to the oven to cook for 3–3½ hours, by which point the meat should be very tender.

Remove the lid, sprinkle the skin with a splash of cider vinegar and a little sea salt and increase the oven temperature back up to 210°C fan/230°C/gas mark 8 to get the crackling crisp. Roast for a further 15–20 minutes. This is good served with buttery garlicky spinach.

Biddenden
Vineyard

Chapel Down

Gusbourne

Simpsons

KENT

Kent has been known as the Garden of England since the sixteenth century when Henry VIII awarded it the epithet after tasting a particularly excellent bowl of its cherries. The county is famed also for hop gardens; oast houses are a feature of the Kentish landscape. Between the wars, many London families exchanged city life for working 'holidays' picking hops, sometimes using stilts to reach the upper bines. Britain's oldest brewery, Shepherd Neame, was founded in Faversham in 1698, although its brewing heritage here is far older.

Kent's other historic delights include the city of Canterbury, with its cathedral and timbered houses, and the castle at Dover on the site of an Iron Age fort.

With an altogether more recent claim to fame is the Vintage Funfair at Dreamland Margate, where the classic boys' outing episode of *Only Fools and Horses* was filmed in 1989. Food lovers are amply catered for with Kentish cobnuts, Whitstable oysters and Romsey Salt Marsh lamb, used by Chef Stephen Harris in the excellent Sportsman Restaurant at Seasalter. In Finglesham near Deal, look for the humorous Ham Sandwich signpost showing the direction to two destinations, one a hamlet, the other a town. Or head to Coxheath for the annual Custard Pie Throwing Championship; or the Isle of Sheppey in the Thames Estuary where the super-sweet Gypsy tart originated.

BIDDENDEN VINEYARDS

Close to the picturesque village of Biddenden in the heart of the Garden of England lies Biddenden Vineyards. Very much a family affair, owned by the Barnes family since 1969, it is Kent's original vineyard on the site of a former apple orchard. Today the Barnes still make delicious ciders (using both cooking and dessert apples for an appealing, more elegant style), including sparkling versions that undergo bottle fermentation, exactly the same process used for sparkling wine

In the late 1960s, the price for English apples was dropping. The germ of an idea to diversify into grape growing came to Joyce Barnes when she heard a feature on Radio Four's *Woman's Hour* about creating vineyards in England. Initially, a third of an acre was planted at their Gribble Bridge Lane property, with their first wine produced in 1973. The rest, as they say, is history. Today it is the second and third generations who run the business with nine hectares now under vines, the furthest being planted no more than 600 metres from the winery, so truly low 'food miles'. At Biddenden, a dozen different varieties are grown including Schönburger, Gewürztraminer and their signature grape Ortega.

The Barnes family like to be innovative and to work with what nature provides, and the result was seen in the startling release in autumn 2021 of their Ortega Late Harvest following the long hot summer of 2018. With a high naturally occurring sweetness (122g of residual sugar in the fruit), this is a ground-breaking style of English dessert wine This is thanks to the experience gained by the family's three generations of winemakers and the current winemaker Tom Barnes' passion for sweet wine, having already successfully developed Biddenden Schönburger. Dessert wines are just one part of the Biddenden range, which encompasses sparkling and still wines, including the gentle, fresh, just off-dry Gribble Bridge White, 100% Ortega, which is a great refreshing summer aperitif wine.

'When I first came back to Biddenden full time in 2011, I noticed a gap in the UK market for sweet wines, with the main focus being on sparkling wines. This led to experimenting with Schönburger — it's a very floral and fruity variety, which lends itself well to a slightly lower abv sweet wine. I'm excited to see this style of wine developing and growing in popularity over the coming years, with Biddenden leading the way in innovation.'

Tom Barnes

FEATURED WINE: **Biddenden Schönburger**. A beguiling varietal dessert wine made from the Schönburger variety, which has deep rose-pink coloured berries and grows well in cool climates, especially those with maritime influence. The grapes are left on the vines, beyond usual harvest date, to be late harvested, so they are picked with higher natural sugar levels. Lots of rich notes of lychee, backed up with honeyed citrus and a bit of gingerbread spice. A great example that England can produce delicious dessert wines.

LOCAL PRODUCE: **Kingcott Blue**, made at Kingcott Dairy just minutes away from Biddenden Vineyards is an unpasteurised soft-centred blue cheese that justly was chosen as Overall Food Product of the Year at the Taste of Kent awards in 2020. It would be delicious with Biddenden's Sparkling Ortega Demi-Sec or even with a glass of their cinnamon and honey-infused Monks Delight Cider – ideal mulled in the winter!

Kentish Apple Tarte Tatin

Although not traditional, using ready-made dulce de leche is easier than making caramel. I have sat through too many traumatic episodes of *The Great British Bake Off* watching bakers in tears – though by all means make the traditional caramel if you prefer. The rich sweetness of the caramel and the buttery pastry matched with vintage sparkling wine is a marriage made in heaven.

SERVES FOUR

320g readymade all-butter puff pastry
15g butter
4 small dessert apples, around 500g, peeled,
*   cored and quartered*
¼ tsp freshly grated nutmeg
¼ tsp ground ginger
Zest and juice of ½ orange
5 tbsp dulce de leche
Mascarpone, to serve

Preheat the oven to 180°C fan/200°C/gas mark 6.

Unroll the pastry on its paper. Place an 18cm plate on top and use a knife to cut round it to make a circle. Lay the pastry circle on the plate, prick it all over and place it in the freezer. (Wrap up the rest of the pastry and freeze it for future use.)

Melt the butter in an 18cm ovenproof frying pan over a medium heat and cook the apple quarters for around 5 minutes until golden.

Mix the spices and orange juice together, pour over the apples and cook for around 1 minute. Spoon the dulce de leche over the top and cook for around 3 minutes until you have a sauce consistency.

(If you're not using an ovenproof frying pan, place the apples into an 18-cm cake tin (not loose-bottomed), snuggling the apple pieces close to each other. Spoon over any leftover dulce de leche. Transfer to the oven for 15 minutes.)

Take the puff pastry from the freezer and lay it on top of the cooked apples, pressing it down on top. Return to the oven and bake for 20–25 minutes until the pastry is puffed up and golden.

Leave to rest for 30 minutes off the heat. Turn out onto a serving dish, sprinkle with the orange zest, slice into quarters and serve with dollops of Mascarpone on the side.

CHAPEL DOWN

One of the most dynamic of English wine estates, Chapel Down has been at the forefront of everything that is most exciting and innovative of English wines since the early 1990s. Rightly so, they are now one of the most recognised brands of English wine for reliable, yet delicious wines with an excellent price to quality ratio. But there is so much more to this producer right across the range, up to and including one of the top cuvée sparkling wines with a considerable price tag, which has already gained a faithful following.

Chapel Down's expansion at their winery close to the small town of Tenterden was swift but well judged – not only from a vinous point of view; they also produce beer, made with the same yeast strain used in champagne, and spirits too, including Bacchus Gin made from distilled grape skins. Currently the largest producer of English wine, Chapel Down is quite unusual in that it is a public listed company.

Apart from owning vineyards in Kent, they source grapes from other counties including Essex and Sussex. But it is their single-vineyard plots that are causing excitement. Kit's Coty Vineyard, a 40-hectare vineyard site in the North Downs, planted in 2007, is seen by winemakers and journalists alike as a shining example of the superb quality levels that Chardonnay can achieve in the UK when given near-perfect growing conditions. But with the recent planting of two similarly favoured plots nearby, Court Lodge and Street Farm are other names to watch under the Chapel Down label.

FEATURED WINE: **Kit's Coty Chardonnay.** A beacon for top-quality English Chardonnay that is destined for still rather than sparkling wine. This award-winning white, fermented with wild yeast, has beautiful richness yet a perfectly judged balance of acidity to make this excellent wine uniquely English in style. Although I have suggested enjoying it with seafood, it is also a perfect partner for roast chicken (flavoured with whole lemon in the cavity as it cooks) or any classic fish dishes, such as sole meunière.

LOCAL PRODUCE: **Oysters from Whitstable** would be fabulous with the Chapel Down Bacchus. If you are not a fan of eating these saline bivalves, but quite like the idea of the taste, you could cheat with Oyster & Vinegar Crisps from Kent Crisps! Or try Winterdale cheese, which is aged in the chalky caves of the North Downs.

Creamy Risotto with Lobster Tails

Risotto must be one of the most relaxing things to cook – the ideal recipe after a stressful day. It might be the act of taking out the day's frustration on chopping the alliums, or the mindful repetitive stirring, or perhaps the glass of wine that is essential for the cook to have in hand.

Although in the world of cookbooks, precise ingredients reign, as I am obliged to write below, but when making risotto at home, my approach is more simplistic. Allow one handful of rice per person and one extra for the saucepan and enough stock as they say in Italian *qb*, which stands for *quanto basta*, meaning 'as needed'. Any good short-grained variety – such as Arborio, Carnaroli or Vialone Nano – is fine but do seek out aged Carnaroli rice from Acquerello, which gives a particular depth to the risotto.

The buttery notes of the Kit's Coty Chardonnay have an affinity with both the lobster and the creaminess of the risotto.

SERVES FOUR

About 1.2 litres chicken or vegetable stock
   (see note opposite)
200g butter, cubed, plus extra for the risotto
1 tbsp olive oil
2 leeks, white parts only, very finely chopped
300g risotto rice
Couple of slugs of Noilly Prat (or any dry vermouth
   or good white wine)
1 large white cauliflower, cut into florets (save the
   leaves for pasta or stir-fry)
Handful of finely grated Parmesan cheese
4 raw lobster tails, shells removed
Finely grated zest of 1 lemon

Warm the stock in a pan and keep over a gentle low heat throughout – do not boil.

Heat a tablespoon each of butter and olive oil in a heavy-based saucepan.

Add the leeks and stir over a low to medium heat for 8 minutes until soft but not coloured.

Toss the rice into the pan and stir continually until all the grains are coated and start to become translucent, about 2 minutes.

Add the vermouth or wine. Keep stirring until evaporated. Then add in two ladlefuls of stock.

Now it's 'Stir, Slurp, Repeat'. Keep stirring well (about every minute or so) and gradually add the stock as the rice expands and cooks. Make sure it does not catch on base of the pan and that there is a glass of wine to hand for the cook to follow the second instruction above!

Add the small florets of cauliflower into the hot stock and cook until very tender (about 8–10 minutes). Remove with slotted spoon and either mash to a rough purée or use a stick blender until smooth.

When the rice is about 5 minutes off being cooked, stir in the cauliflower purée – you can add more stock afterwards as needed, but adding at this stage means it is easier to judge the consistency of the final risotto.

After about 18–20 minutes, taste the rice: it should be soft, not squidgy, but keeping its shape – you may need another 5 minutes. Remove from the heat. Add a generous knob of butter and the Parmesan and start the workout known to the Italians as the *mantecatura* – basically beating it vigorously for 3–4 minutes – your arms may start to complain at this point. This creates the creamy texture of the risotto.

When the risotto is about 8 minutes from being ready, prepare the lobster tails. Put 3–4 tablespoons of cold water in a large frying pan and heat to a simmer. Gradually add in the 200g cubed butter. Melt over a low heat (otherwise the water and butter will separate). Add the raw lobster tails and baste continually with the butter until cooked – about 6–8 minutes. If you have a meat thermometer their internal temperature should reach 60°C. They can be held in the butter for a few minutes and the risotto likewise can sit happily off the heat for a few minutes, so do not panic if one is ready a couple of minutes before the other.

Serve the risotto in warmed pasta bowls, with the poached lobster tails on top, some grated lemon zest and drizzle over a little of the cooking butter.

PS – Without wanting to sound bossy, using homemade stock makes all the difference to the flavours in your risotto. If you have never made your own (lack of time/inclination), please do give it a go – it takes minutes after a roast chicken lunch to throw the bones and some chopped veg into a pot, cover with water – no need to add salt – but feel free to throw in any aromatics you have to hand: parsley stalks, fresh herbs, the odd bay leaf, some peppercorns… Gently simmer then cool, sieve and stash in the freezer for later. Plus there's the feelgood factor of using leftovers. The liquid packets available in supermarkets will do but please: no stock cubes (if in doubt why not recommended, just read the ingredients list on the packet).

Also, although the rich buttery lobster works well, if the price seems a little excessive for supper on a Tuesday, you could do with buttered large prawns instead – look out for MSC-approved, UK-grown, cold water prawns.

GUSBOURNE

The original Gusbourne Estate dates back as far as 1410 and was owned by the de Goosebournes, whose family crest featured three geese, which are still reflected in the Gusbourne logo. But its current embodiment as a modern wine estate began in 2004. South African-born Andrew Weeber planted vines on this rather surprising spot, just a few miles north of the English Channel. Why surprising? Because Appledore is close to the wet marshes rather than the more obviously suited chalky North Downs of Kent. Indeed, their property is bordered by the Royal Military Canal, constructed during the Napoleonic Wars. The soil is compacted Wealden clay on Tunbridge Wells sandy loam – not the usual habitat for growing grapes – but the resulting sparkling wines have wonderful deep flavours and have more than justified Andrew's choice of location.

The estate has undergone quite a transformation since its foundation. Head winemaker Charlie Holland is also CEO, with Jim Ormonde as Chairman. They have also been joined by majority investors, most notably Lord Ashcroft (also known for his spectacular collection of Victoria Cross medals). As well as their plantings on the original site, they also have about a third of their total vines planted near Goodwood in West Sussex. Gusbourne only use grapes from their own vineyards and solely the classic trilogy of champagne varieties.

Gusbourne's philosophy is a quest for perfection through their fastidious approach to detail. They focus on only vintage wines, so they can allow the unique character of each year's harvest to show through. Their approach to winemaking is quite unforgiving in the pursuit of brilliance. Charlie, who has been recognised three times as English Wine Producer of the Year, is patient and meticulous and this is reflected in the style of wines. As well as the featured wine below, do look out for their Sparkling Blanc de Blancs, which displays a linear purity as well as richness, and has quite a pedigree, having been served at the launch of the London Olympics in 2012 and at Buckingham Palace.

'At Gusbourne, we embrace tradition but readily challenge convention, even to make what might seem like very small differences to the finished wine. Attention to detail is often the difference between great and exceptional.'
Charlie Holland

FEATURED WINE: **Boot Hill Pinot Noir**. Named after the vineyard which, when viewed on a map, looks like a boot, which is planted with both Chardonnay and Pinot Noir. Lauded by many a wine journalist as England's answer to burgundy, it has its own distinct English character. Basketfuls of red cherries on the nose, with an underlying pepperiness, ripe tannins and a touch of smoke make this a serious Pinot Noir.

LOCAL PRODUCE: **Romney Salt Marsh Lamb**, produced from the Romney breed that is grazed on the natural grasses and samphire that give the meat a very distinctive sweet yet rich flavour. Look out also for Shaggy's Beard, a Camembert-style ripened goat's cheese from Ellie's Dairy based in the North Downs of the county.

Goose Gratin

One of those warming, autumnal dishes, which traditionally took an endless amount of time to prepare, this version takes advantage of those wonderful jars of goose confit for a speedier supper. Normally picked up on shopping jaunt to France, there is an excellent supplier near Exeter in Devon, Pipers Farm, that sustainably raises geese. If you cannot lay your hands on *confit d'oie*, then duck confit will work just as well. It is equally a great way to use up any left-over goose, or indeed duck, after a roast. You can also play around with the beans and opt for cannellini or butter beans instead of haricot.

Given that the family crest of the Gusbourne Estate is three geese, and that Boot Hill Pinot Noir with goose is a match made in heaven, this pairing has a certain synergy! I did struggle with advising how many this should feed, because goose is quite rich, but it is also so moreish. It reheats happily the next day and can be mixed through some grains for a warm salad.

SERVES THREE TO FOUR (OR TWO HUNGRY BODS
IN OUR HOUSEHOLD AFTER A COUNTRY WALK!)

2 confit goose legs
1 large white onion, finely chopped
3 thyme sprigs, leaves picked
1 rosemary sprig, leaves picked
1 bay leaf
720g jar of white haricot beans (El Navarrico's alubias blanco are excellent), drained and rinsed thoroughly
200ml homemade stock (vegetable or chicken)
2 larges slices of sourdough, toasted and blitzed to medium coarse breadcrumbs
1 tsp dry English mustard powder (optional)
Sea salt and black pepper

Remove the goose legs from the fridge about an hour before you start to cook.

Preheat the oven to 180°C fan/200°C/ gas mark 6. Place the legs on a baking tray. Remove most of the fat – keep it for another recipe (awesome for roast potatoes). Bake for about 20 minutes until totally heated through (check the pack for recommended timings).

Meanwhile, heat a little of the goose fat in a large frying pan and cook the onion until soft but not coloured – about 8 minutes.

Sprinkle in the thyme and rosemary and add the bay leaf, along with the beans. Season and add the stock. Allow to bubble away slowly to reduce the stock for 15 minutes; it should be almost all absorbed into the beans.

Remove the goose from the oven and shred using two forks. You may want to discard the skin, or you can make it into crunchy snacks later by baking at 190°C fan/210°C/gas mark 7 for 20 minutes or so.

Add the goose meat to the bean mixture and stir well. Divide between two shallow dishes or four ramekins. Mix the sourdough breadcrumbs with the mustard powder (if using) and generously cover the goose mixture. Bake in the oven on a baking tray for 15–20 minutes until coloured. Serve in the dishes – warn your guests that it is hot! – possibly with a crisp endive salad on the side, dressed with raspberry vinaigrette to echo the red fruit notes of the wine.

SIMPSONS WINE ESTATE

Ruth and Charles Simpson have come to making English wine in Kent via a rather unusual and circuitous route, having bought a wine estate in the Languedoc in 2002. At their French domaine, Sainte Rose, they produce an eclectic range of award-winning wines, still and sparkling. This initial foray into wine production – albeit in southern France, with its entirely different climate – meant that in 2012 they could hit the ground running in the UK. Applying their personal brand of *savoir-faire* (the 'not to do' as much as the 'how to do' rules), the Simpsons work on combining the best of old and new worlds of wine, using state of the art modern technology to bring out the nuances and sense of place in their wines.

In the picturesque, AONB-designated Elham Valley in the North Downs, the vineyard is sited on the same band of chalk that underlies the Champagne region of France. It is also one of the sunniest spots in England, with a good but not excessive temperature variation between day and night – ideal for adding to the complexity of flavour. The Simpsons only vinify grapes from their own vines, and are applying the same level of hands-on attention to detail, from soil analysis to rootstock selection, with the aim of producing great wines that reflect the *terroir* of this part of Kent.

Although Simpsons make excellent sparkling wines (from the traditional trio of varieties), and despite Charles having sworn never to make a still red from Pinot Noir, the bountiful vintage of 2018 saw the launch of their Rabbit Hole Pinot Noir, a delightful fragrant Pinot that takes time to develop in the glass. Also worth seeking out is their Derringstone Pinot Meunier (this red grape is vinified here as a still white wine), as is their other still white, The Roman Road Chardonnay. The 2018 vintage of this, their flagship wine, received the highest accolade of 'Best in Show' in the 2020 Decanter World Wine Awards.

'As keen consumers of wine and having travelled to many wine-producing areas of the world, it was a spirit of adventure and a desire to be part of positive change that took Charles and I initially to France. It began with an aspiration to help transform the reputation of the Languedoc from a low quality, high volume wine producer to a high quality, low volume wine producer, a challenge that continues to this day. That same desire to be part of an emerging and evolving area was what also brought us back to the UK, our aspiration this time to help drive the extraordinary development that has seen England and Wales grow from being a little known and insignificant wine producer, to the most exciting and dynamic wine producing area in the world.

Since we established Simpsons' Wine Estate in 2012, it is going from strength to strength. The initial plan was to produce solely Classic Method English Sparkling Wine, however the incredible harvest of 2018 inspired the creation of the Simpsons' range of sensational still wines.'

Ruth Simpson

FEATURED WINE: **Railway Hill Rosé**. Presented in an attractive shaped bottle, with a glass Vinolok stopper (meaning the entire bottle can be recycled or repurposed), this pale, elegant Provençal-style pink is named after the light railway that traversed what is now the Simpsons' Railway Hill Vineyard, linking Canterbury to Folkestone in the late nineteenth century. This is an excellent expression of a varietal Pinot Noir rosé with a lovely nose of pink grapefruit and redcurrants. One word of advice: always put a second bottle in the fridge at the same time as you open the first!

LOCAL PRODUCE: A platter from the fabulous salami and other cured meats from **Moons Green Charcuterie** near Tenterden – either their saucisson with wild mushroom and truffle or with venison, sour cherries and pistachio nuts would be lovely as an aperitif with a glass of their sparkling rosé, Canterbury Rose.

Tuna and Fennel Meatballs with Bucatini

My first encounter with these delicious 'meatballs' was over a lazy lunch, where a battalion of wine bottles seemed to be endlessly appearing, on a vine-covered terrace on the beautiful island of Salina, off the north coast of Sicily. You could replace the bucatini in this recipe with spaghetti or linguine. I am a great fan of rosé wine with food, but for me they must be rosés with character, not light, monodimensional quaffing styles. The featured wine from Simpsons ticks all the boxes on character and with the tuna, it is delectable.

SERVES FOUR

2 red peppers

500g cherry tomatoes, halved

Olive oil, for drizzling

Small bunch of fresh basil

400g fresh tuna steak, diced into 2cm pieces

55g pine kernels, toasted

Handful of flat-leaf parsley, chopped

2 tsp fennel seeds, dry-toasted and pounded to
    a medium powder

1 tsp dried oregano

100g panko breadcrumbs

25g Parmesan cheese, grated

2 free-range eggs

Zest and juice of 1 lemon

320g bucatini

Sea salt and black pepper

Preheat the oven to 180°C fan/200°C/gas mark 6. Put the whole red peppers on a baking tray and roast for about 45 minutes until soft and the skins start to colour. Lay the cherry tomatoes, cut side up, on a separate baking tray. Drizzle with olive oil and sprinkle with salt. Roast for about 25 minutes until starting to char on the edges. Remove both trays and allow to cool.

Once cool, skin and deseed the peppers, keeping as much of the roasting juice as possible. Chop roughly and put into the jug of a stick blender. Add the roasted tomatoes, including all the charred bits, about 8–10 large basil leaves and blitz to a purée. (This can be done the day before and kept in the fridge.)

Meanwhile, heat a couple of glugs of olive oil in a large frying pan and add the tuna and pine kernels. Season and fry briefly, stirring, so that the fish is coloured on all sides. Tip into a bowl and leave to cool for 10 minutes.

Add the parsley, fennel seeds, oregano, breadcrumbs, Parmesan, eggs and the lemon zest and juice. Time to get your hands in and squidge all the mixture together until fully amalgamated. Shape into small balls, about the size of a large walnut. Place on a baking tray lined with baking paper and chill in the fridge for an hour or so.

Bring a large saucepan of salted water to the boil and cook the bucatini following the packet instructions. Put the tomato and pepper sauce into a large frying pan, heat very gently over a low heat – you want to want to keep the fresh flavour so do not boil.

Heat some olive oil in another large frying pan and brown the meatballs, moving them around until coloured on all sides.

Drop the meatballs into the warm sauce to
finish cooking (about 10 minutes). Add in the
cooked, drained pasta and gently combine,
adding a spoonful of pasta cooking water to
slacken the sauce if needed. Serve in warm
bowls, topped with a little chopped basil.

THE CHEESE SHED

Harrow & Hope

Windsor Great Park

High Clandon

Litmus

BUCKINGHAMSHIRE, BERKSHIRE AND SURREY

Space constraints mean that we can only include a fraction of the 800 or so vineyards in England – and vineyards have been planted from Gloucestershire to Yorkshire, Somerset to Norfolk. Many of the vineyards are growers who supply their fruit to other winemakers, and so you may well find that a sparkling wine made in Hampshire might include grapes sourced from Essex as well. So here are just four final wine producers to fly the flag for the other English wine counties featuring Surrey, Buckinghamshire and Berkshire.

HARROW & HOPE

Growing up in a wine family, with a famous, instantly recognisable surname, did not automatically mean that Henry Laithwaite would follow in his parents' vinous footsteps. His father Tony started his own wine company in 1969, which broke the mould of the traditional British wine trade, and his mother Barbara has her own vineyard in Oxfordshire – Wyfold. But through various spells working vintages in Australia, the Rhône and Bordeaux, Henry discovered that wine really did flow through his veins, becoming a winemaker aged just 17.

After living and making wine in Bordeaux he and his wife Kaye (along with their young family) decided to head back to the UK to devote themselves to producing sparkling wine. In 2010, they chose a 6.5 hectare site for their vineyard in Buckinghamshire, on a former gravel terrace of the Thames, close to the lovely town of Marlow in the Chiltern Hills. This beautiful location, with high daytime temperatures and cooler nights that preserve the acidity in the grapes, is what gave rise to the estate's name, owing to the harrow-mangling flint in its soils. Harrow & Hope produce wines that truly reflect their terroir: since the 2019 vintage, their barrel-aged wines only use the yeasts that naturally occur in the H&H vineyards – that really does give a sense of place.

Henry has the great combination of hopeful pragmatism. He focuses on a natural and sustainable method of production, as far as Mother Nature allows, with more than a fair nod to the biodynamic ethos of Rudolf Steiner. He has also inherited the family work ethic, along with a mongoose-like curiosity to find out more and always experiment.

Very deservedly past winners of Winery of the Year award, H&H make four excellent different sparkling wines: a Classic blend, a Rosé, a Blanc de Blancs and a Blanc de Noirs. The last is delightful, with layers of flavour that just keep on unveiling and developing in the glass.

'I feel both excitement and nervousness about the direction H&H is going in. But this is par for the course in what we do. Jumping into organics is a step into the unknown, but ever since I started making wine and growing grapes I've always had an innate belief that nature knows what to do, we just need to give her a gentle helping hand. Making wines that taste of where they come from is the ultimate goal for us, whilst making sure that what we produce gives people great pleasure and enhances any occasion.'

Henry Laithwaite

FEATURED WINE: **Blanc de Blancs.** For their Blanc de Blancs, Harrow & Hope use the same organically farmed, chalk plot where their Chardonnay really shines, and each year the wine has 50% barrel fermentation and 40 months on the lees, which gives a lovely depth of concentration and complexity. Although each vintage is different, there is a similar style that comes through each year's unique variance.

The wine is a glorious blend of citrus and creaminess – think of the flavour profile of a lemon meringue pie!

LOCAL PRODUCE: **Bix**, an irresistible triple cream cheese from the Nettlebed Creamery near Henley-on-Thames, is excellent with the H&H Sparkling Rosé Vintage Brut.

Poached Pheasant with Parsnip, Pistachio and Bulgur Wheat Salad

Because Harrow & Hope wines always remind me of happy times and celebrations, it's only too easy to think about enjoying a glass on its own… or maybe with some avocado and prawn tartlets… and it's heavenly with prawn toasts as a way to start the weekend. But this delicious warm salad of delicate poached pheasant with sweet parsnips is a lovely match. The nuttiness of the bulgur wheat complements the Blanc de Blancs. Tart pomegranate seeds give a lovely lift to the dish and while I find it soothing to attack the halved fruit with a wooden spoon to loosen the seeds, if you prefer not to splatter your kitchen surfaces with red juice, then just buy prepared seeds. If you are short on time, you could replace the pheasant with slices of smoked duck breast from Weald Smokery.

SERVES FOUR

4 small/baby parsnips, peeled and cut into roughly
   3cm cubes
75ml olive oil, plus extra for roasting
1 tsp ground sumac
120g bulgur wheat (or wholemeal giant couscous or
   red quinoa)
150ml boiling water
About 1.5 litres chicken stock, homemade if possible
2 star anise
1 tsp fennel seeds

4 skinless pheasant breasts
Large bunch of watercress, leaves picked
Large handful of flat-leaf parsley, chopped
Large handful of shelled pistachios, chopped
Extra-virgin olive oil, for drizzling
Sherry vinegar, for drizzling
Seeds from 1 pomegranate – no pith!
Sea salt flakes

Preheat the oven to 180°C fan/200°C/gas mark 6.

Put the prepared parsnip on a baking tray, drizzle with olive oil and scatter over the sumac. Toss to coat then roast for about 15–20 minutes until soft and starting to caramelise, turning once.

Heat a dry frying pan and add the bulgur wheat, turning until it smells toasty (about 3 minutes). Remove from the heat and tip into a shallow bowl (a pasta bowl is ideal). Add in the measured olive oil and enough boiling water to cover the grains. Leave to soak for 20 minutes before fluffing up with a fork to separate the grains.

Meanwhile, heat the chicken stock with the star anise and fennel seeds in a large saucepan. Add the pheasant breasts and ensure they are immersed in the stock: pour in extra boiling water if more liquid is needed. Cover with a lid and poach the meat over a medium heat for about 12–15 minutes until cooked.

To plate up, mix the bulgur wheat with the watercress, parsley and pistachios. Dress with extra-virgin olive oil, sea salt flakes and sherry vinegar. Slice the drained pheasant breasts on the diagonal into thick slices and drape artistically on the salad and sprinkle with pomegranate seeds.

HIGH CLANDON

Drinking retsina on board a stylish 1930s windjammer under full sail around the islands of the Peloponnese is not perhaps what one thinks of in relation to English wine. But it was while working on board that memorable wine cruise that I first met the charming owners of High Clandon vineyard, Sibylla and Bruce Tindale. Both South African born, they planted the classic trio of Chardonnay, Pinot Noir and Pinot Meunier vines in the picturesque flint and chalky Surrey Hills in 2004. It's a delightful spot along a wooded country lane between Guildford and Dorking, protected as an Area of Outstanding Natural Beauty, but with stunning views of the City of London skyline. It is not only home to vines but also a truffle wood, planted with hazels and oaks. There is a beautiful wildflower meadow that is nectar heaven for their own bees. The Tindales are also lovers of art, and the property hosts visiting artists with dramatic sculptures dotted among the wildflower meadow.

High Clandon is no vanity project or a pet hobby, Sibylla and Bruce are very much hands on, working hard throughout the year on this boutique vineyard. Both studied winemaking and viticulture at Plumpton in East Sussex and they make a good team, working alternate vine rows in their own style. Their cossetted grapes are transformed into wine by the inspirational winemaker that is Emma Rice (of Hattingley Valley). They have a philosophy of creating a quintessential English sparkling wine and only release vintage cuvées rather than non-vintage wines.

Their range of sparkling wines include the Euphoria Cuvée, which has an enticing note of buttery flapjack, and the award-winning Elysium, which spends six years on the lees giving the wine depth of complexity alongside all the classic autolytic notes of brioche and toast, as well as ripe apricots. For something a little different, do look out for their Cupid Blue Gin, distilled from their own Eau de Vie, and named in honour of a rare Blue Butterfly (*Cupido minimus* for any lepidopterist readers who want to know!).

'Bruce and I adore it when our visitors relish our celebrated Tour, Talk, Tasting and especially when we can tutor them to be a successful sabrageur. So far, a 100% record of success with the sabre! A tale to tell. A marvellous 95-year-old lady — one of the celebrated women who flew Spitfires in WW2 from factory to airfield during the Battle of Britain — visited in June 2021 as she was celebrating her forthcoming 95th birthday (as it happens a day before The Queen's 95th) — and we asked if she would like to do a sabrage. 'Yes' she responded with alacrity and with such panache, wielded the sabre and with her first flourish off flew the champagne cork. Now that's chutzpah. And the result: she received our Certificate of Achievement.'

Sibylla Tindale

FEATURED WINE: **Halcyon Vintage Cuvée**. The house style of allowing long maturation — almost five years ageing on the lees for this wine — gives a depth and complexity to this exceptionally food-friendly fizz. Just over half the blend is Chardonnay, the rest naturally the other duo of the Holy Trinity of Champenoise varieties. There is fresh tropical fruit on the nose, leading into biscuit and brioche notes. The next five-year aged vintage, named The Elizabethan Cuvée 2017, has been created to celebrate the Queen's Platinum Jubilee in 2022.

LOCAL PRODUCE: **Floyd Cheese**, a soft washed-rind cheese from the Gimblett Cheese Company in Haslemere, is delicious on its own on crackers or whipped with grated truffles and served with glazed shallots. It's glorious matched with the Elysium.

Sibylla's Truffle Gougères

This recipe is one of Sibylla's own – and one she cooks regularly to welcome visitors to the estate – which goes so well with their style of sparkling wine. It's a great way to use the truffles from their own truffle wood, which they find using their own dogs as truffle hounds!

MAKES 35–40 GOUGÈRES

For the gougères:
90g plain flour
½ tsp mustard powder
Pinch of mild curry powder
2 large eggs
70g good English Cheddar cheese – such as Sussex
    Charmer
70g butter
150ml water
Sea salt and black pepper

For the truffle cream filling:
Black Sussex truffles – about 50g – depending on
    the intensity required
200g cream cheese
3 tbsp double cream

Preheat the oven to 200°C fan/220°C/gas mark 7 and place a deep baking tray of water onto the base of the oven.

To make the choux pastry, ideally use a hand-held electric whisk, and have everything ready before starting.

Put the flour, mustard powder and mild curry powder into a small bowl and grind over 7 twists each of salt and pepper.

Beat the eggs into a separate bowl.

Grate the Cheddar cheese into a third bowl.

Put the butter with the measured water into a saucepan and bring to the boil. Take off the heat and shoot in the flour, whisking briskly to rapidly incorporate air, until it forms a ball coming away from the edge of the pan (about 30 seconds!)

Beat the eggs vigorously into the flour mixture, a little at a time, until you have a glossy paste. Add and stir in the grated cheese.

Dampen a large, greased 40 × 30cm baking sheet with a sprinkle of water, and then spoon onto it teaspoon-sized lumps of choux.

Bake for 10 minutes on the middle shelf of the oven, then bake for a further 10 minutes on the top shelf until golden. Allow to cool well.

To make the filling, peel the truffle lightly, reserving the black outer skin for mixing into the cream.

Grate the truffle and mix the remaining filling ingredients.

Add ½ tablespoon of filling to each gougère once it is cooled – or piping it in is rather efficient!

LITMUS WINES

Litmus Wines is an English wine company like no other: purveyors of a host of winemaking services – contract winemakers, wine business consultants, contract growers, importer, distributor and supplier of biotechnical kit to the wine industry. They do not own any of their own vineyards but contract grapes from across the south of England.

Litmus is the winemaking team that looks after the 88-hectare vineyard owned by Denbies Wine Estate in Dorking, Surrey, and its wine production. It was started as a separate personal project in 2008 by Australian-born John Worontschak. John has been making wine in England since 1988, but has always offered winemaking consultancy around the world and continues to, which gives him a great overview of trends in the wine world (several of which he started himself!).

With a can-do, somewhat maverick attitude, John is excited by the possibilities in the English wine industry today. The limitations are far less than in traditional wine-producing countries, giving winemakers far more freedom, added to the fact of warmer weather patterns and a greater understanding of what is planted and where. The style is to use older barrels as well as allowing more time on the lees to increase complexity – the aim is for wines that have good structure and to be extremely food friendly.

In 2010, Litmus launched Element 20, a blend of Chardonnay and Bacchus, and now also offers three other still wines: a White Pinot (entirely Pinot Noir grapes that are vinified as a white), a Pinot Noir and an orange Bacchus. But do look out as well for their Ginking – a blend of London dry gin, English wine and sparkling water – for relaxed summer drinking.

'I am very proud of the Litmus Wines range and the great success we are having with them. They are vinous proof that English wines are capable of being so much more than light and pretty and can be complex wines full of interest for the table, holding their own with the best of them.'

John Worontschak

FEATURED WINE: **Litmus 20**. The first wine released is an elegant interpretation of Chardonnay and Bacchus with excellent oak management that supports the wine without overpowering it: think white burgundy in style, with very pure fruit. The label features a coccolith, an ancient sea creature with a calcium shell that is a component of the chalky soils of southern England.

LOCAL PRODUCE: **Dirty Vicar Cheese**, a Camembert-esque cow's milk cheese, from the same artisan maker of Norbury Blue, based in Albury, near the Litmus HQ. Or try the fabulous charcuterie from Tempus Foods with the Litmus Pinot Noir!

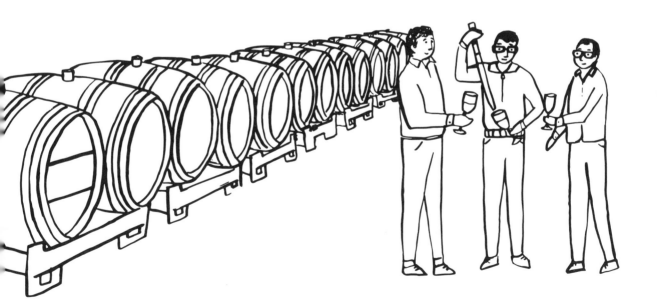

Chicken with Anchovies and Rosemary with Hazelnut Gremolata

An outstanding match for this complex white wine is a simple roast chicken, with no more than lashings of soft butter on the skin and good sprinkles of crunchy sea salt flakes. But the multi-layered flavours of this wine can happily snuggle up to some quite punchy flavours, as in this recipe.

If you aren't a lover of anchovies, don't worry as this marvellous addition simply adds a depth of flavour rather than any intrinsic fishiness. I've often used anchovies in my roast lamb, without telling the anchovy-hating member of my family who always finishes their plate. I was inspired to try it with chicken from another recipe in the brilliant Diana Henry's book *A Bird in the Hand*. I've reworked her recipe slightly as the addition of a hazelnut gremolata gives an added dimension reflecting the oak ageing of the paired wine.

SERVES FOUR

Olive oil, for browning
8 large chicken thighs, skin on
8 banana shallots, peeled and quartered lengthways
4 garlic cloves, crushed
5 anchovies, drained from tin and chopped
80ml dry white wine
Zest and juice of 1 lemon
2 rosemary sprigs, leaves picked and chopped

168

Large handful of toasted hazelnuts, finely chopped
Large handful of flat-leaf parsley, finely chopped

Preheat the oven to 180°C fan/200°C/gas mark 6.

Heat two glugs of olive oil in a heavy casserole pan over a medium heat. Brown the chicken thighs briefly on each side and remove to a plate. (I cook the chicken bone in but you can cook bone out if you have fussy eaters – just reduce the overall cooking time by about 5 minutes.)

Add the shallots to the pan and cook for about 3 minutes to colour. Turn the heat to low and add three of the crushed garlic cloves and the anchovies. Cook for a few more minutes: do not let the garlic burn and press the anchovies down with a spoon so that they soften into a paste.

Add the wine, lemon juice and the rosemary, stir very briefly and remove from the heat so that it doesn't catch. Place the chicken on top of the shallot mixture, skin-side up. Transfer to the oven to bake, uncovered, for 35 minutes.

Meanwhile, make the gremolata. Mix together the last garlic clove, lemon zest, the toasted hazelnuts and parsley.

To check the chicken is ready, use a meat thermometer: it should read 65°C when inserted into the thickest part of the thigh, or pierce the meat and check that the juices run clear.

Serve on warmed plates and sprinkle the chicken with generous amounts of gremolata. Good with buttered spinach and Jersey Royals.

WINDSOR GREAT PARK VINEYARD

The Great Park that spreads out to the south of the Royal Residence of Windsor Castle, with its iconic three-mile-long, tree-lined avenue and Deer Park, is not perhaps where one would expect to find a vineyard. But tucked away, a small distance from the public areas of the park, in a spectacular location overlooking Great Meadow Pond, is a perfect sand-and-clay-soil plot that is home to a unique English wine.

In fact, there were vines planted in the Great Park as far back as the 12th century. Jump nine centuries and, since 2011, there have been three hectares of the noble champagne varieties of Chardonnay, Pinot Noir and Pinot Meunier, with the white grapes making up 55% of the planting. And it all happened by chance.

Anne Linder, head buyer at Laithwaites at the time, took a call from a Windsor shop customer, the former Governor General of the Military Knights at Windsor Castle, Sir Michael Hobbs. He had a small complaint... which led to a chat and a visit to the castle. Anne took a bottle of Theale English Sparkling as a gift and was given a tour of the gardens. She pointed out a grassy slope that, she quipped, would be great for vines. And so, the germ of this incredible idea was sown.

The ethos of Windsor Great Park and its ranger, then the late Duke of Edinburgh, is to champion all that is essentially English, including rare breeds and traditional crop varieties, with biodiversity front of mind. Laithwaites already had a strong track record in producing excellent English fizz and they promised that the wine from this very special location would be the very best it could be.

Permission was granted and Laithwaites became tenant farmers of The Crown Estate, with the vines planted in 2011. Their first vintage was 2013, released in 2016 — nothing ever happens quickly in a vineyard!

With its delightful bubbles, crisp red apples and toasty fruit on the nose, this limited-production fizz invites you in before you even sip it. Perfect as an aperitif or with lunch at a quintessential English summer garden party.

But it is not just about the wine – delicious and multi-award-winning though that is — the vineyard is also an important community project, involving local groups, schools and staff from Laithwaites. Quite some achievement.

'English bubbly reaches a new peak of excitement with this first release from Windsor Great Park.'

Hugh Johnson, on tasting the vintage of 2013, which was released in 2017.

FEATURED WINE: **Windsor Great Park Sparkling**. This limited-production sparkling has delightful bubbles, and beautiful bright citrus fruit and crisp red apples on the nose, which lead into a mélange of hazelnut, apricots and toast. With its toasty notes it invites you in – perfect as an aperitif or with lunch at a quintessential English summer garden party.

LOCAL PRODUCE: **Waterloo Cheese**, made in Berkshire, by the Wigmore family. Originally made from the milk from a herd on the Duke of Wellington's estate, hence the name. Today, still made from Guernsey cattle, near Henley on Thames.

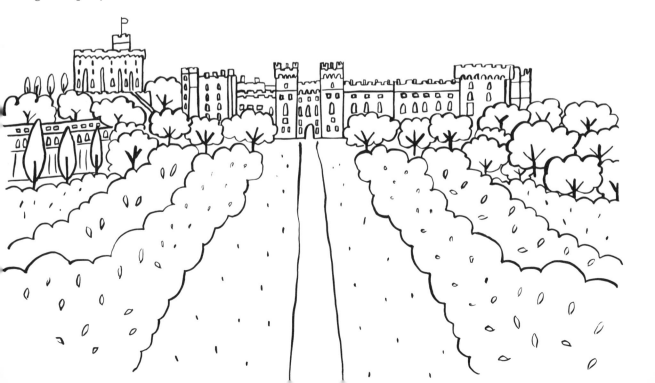

Salmon Coulibiac

Although this wonderful wine would sit very happily with a simple platter of smoked salmon – and maybe alongside scrambled eggs for brunch – a slightly more sophisticated recipe is called for to honour this sparkling English vinous royalty.

Originally Russian, the dish was reinvented by the renowned French chef, Escoffier. I have provided a simplified version as the original involves making a brioche dough, crêpes, a velouté sauce and more, but this version tastes just as regal.

SERVES FOUR

1 tbsp olive oil, plus extra to drizzle

2 tbsp of butter

30g shallot, finely diced

½ small bulb of fennel (around 75g), diced

80g basmati and wild rice

1 tsp ground fennel

200ml hot water

1 tbsp Verjus *

1 tbsp each chopped flat-leaf parsley and dill or fennel fronds

400g piece salmon, skin on

320g readymade all-butter puff pastry

1 egg, beaten, for glazing

Sea salt and black pepper

(* Verjus is the juice pressed from unripe grapes and is a fabulous ingredient that adds a burst of sharp tang to a dish, whilst more subtle than vinegar or lemon juice. English Verjus is available from Verjuice, based in Ditchling. If you cannot get hold of any, apple cider vinegar can be used as a substitute.)

Heat the oil and butter in a pan and add the diced shallot and fennel. Season and cook over a low heat for 5–7 minutes until starting to soften.

Add the rice and ground fennel seeds and cook for 1 minute. Season again and then pour in the hot water. Cover with a lid, turn the heat down to low and simmer for about 20 minutes until the rice is tender. Stir in the verjus and herbs and spoon onto a large plate to cool.

While the rice is cooking, heat a little oil in a large frying pan and pan-fry the salmon, skin-side down, for 1 minute then turn over and turn off the heat. Let the salmon sit in the pan for 1 minute to lightly cook, then carefully transfer to a plate to cool before peeling off the skin.

Preheat the oven to 200°C fan/220°C/gas mark 7 and preheat a baking sheet.

Once the rice and salmon are completely cool, unroll the pastry on its paper with its longest side nearest you. Roll it out lightly until it measures about 25cm deep and 36cm wide. Score down the middle to make two rectangles around 25 × 18cm.

Spoon half the rice onto the left-hand rectangle of pastry, leaving a 1cm border around the edge, then top with the peeled salmon fillet. Cover with the rest of the rice and season again.

Fold the right-hand rectangle of pastry over the left and fold over the edges of the pastry to seal.

Use a sharp knife to score the top of the pastry very lightly, but make sure you don't cut all the way through. Glaze with the egg.

Slide the paper onto the warmed baking sheet and bake in the oven for 15 minutes, then turn the heat down to 180°C fan/200°C/ gas mark 6, and continue to bake for another 10 minutes.

Use a serrated knife to cut into four pieces and serve.

URBAN WINERIES

An urban winery? Is it not all about the bucolic beauty of a vineyard, gleaming row after row of vines on an English summer's day? And where do they get the grapes?

Just a few thoughts that run through people's minds when they learn that as of 2022, there are at least four notable urban wineries in London, and more set to pop up quickly, both in the Capital and elsewhere across the country. Gateshead is home to the **Laneberg Winery**, where winemaker Elise Lane has made Fortnum & Mason's own-label Bacchus at the first urban winery in Tyneside.

In 2013, London's first urban winery – **London Cru** – was opened by respected wine importer Roberson Wine. Based in a former gin distillery near Earls Court, as well as making wines, they offer London visitors and residents the opportunity to learn more about winemaking right on their doorstep. The early vintages were made from grapes sourced from Europe, but since 2017 their wines are made from grapes grown in West Sussex and the South of England.

Sergio Verillo built up his impressive vinous CV working in New Zealand, Burgundy, South Africa and California to name a few of the regions in which he has made wine. Since 2017 he and his wife Lyndsey have been making wine under the **Blackbook** label at a railway arch in Battersea, London. Sourcing grapes from Essex, Surrey, Kent and Oxfordshire for their flagship varietals of Chardonnay and Pinot Noir the Verillos also make quirky but delicious one-off experimental wines.

A near-neighbour of Blackbook, inside the iconic towers of the Battersea Power Station redevelopment, **Vagabond Urban Winery** have been making around 25,000 bottles each year since 2017. Their focus is on English wines using grapes sourced from Essex, Surrey and Oxfordshire that can compete on the international wine market. They produce a zingy Bacchus as well as a sparkling Pét Nat, which has been joined by a zingy Pét Nat called Pét Not, made from Pinot grapes, all of which are available in their eight London wine bars as well as from the winery. Winemaker Gavin Monery sees that the natural acidity in English grapes gives the opportunity to make these more approachable, fun styles of fizz.

Bethnal Green in the East End is home to **Renegade**, started in 2016 by Warwick Smith and Josh Hammond, who source many varieties of grapes everywhere from Sussex to southern Italy, Spain and Germany. They produce a wide range of wines, including a bubbly Bacchus and Bethnal Bubbles – a dry hopped sparkling wine made from English Solaris grapes.

VISITING ENGLISH VINEYARDS

WineGB (*winegb.co.uk*) lists the UK's vineyards by region/county as well as estates that are open to visitors. It's advisable to call in advance about a tasting visit unless any specifically have a cellar door/tasting room open daily. Several have on-site restaurants or cafés or the option to pick up a bottle at their cellar door and enjoy a picnic in their vineyards.

It would be very remiss not to mention that Wales, although obviously a separate country and an immensely proud one at that, is home to more than thirty vineyards that are listed on the WineGB website.

WineGB's other regional associations include:

WineGB East
WineGB Midlands & North
WineGB South East
WineGB South
WineGB Wessex
WineGB West

Other regional vineyard associations that are a great source of information for visiting vineyards include:

surreyhillsvineyards.co.uk
sussexwineries.co.uk
vineyardsofhampshire.co.uk
winegardenofengland.co.uk

Staying on a Vineyard

Such is the interest and investment in English vineyards that new places to stay are popping up all the time. From an eco pod for a romantic weekend in the middle of the vines to cottages and cabins as well as pubs and luxury hotels not far from the wine estates, do visit the WineGB website for details. Or, for a private English wine tour visiting some of the most exciting estates and staying in fabulous locations, do get in touch via my website: *www.lovewinefood.com*.

Where to Buy English Wines

Often the best place to buy is directly from the wine estate, either by calling in for a tasting at the cellar door or ordering directly from them online. If you have yet to try any of the wines and want to taste a selection across the range, if any estate does not offer mixed cases, do contact one of the independent merchants who specialise in English wines. Their knowledge is excellent, and they are more than happy to suggest wines that fit with your taste and budget.

Hawkins Brothers – *www.hawkinsbros.co.uk*

The English Wine Collection – *www.theenglishwinecollection.co.uk*

Grape Britannia – *www.grapebritannia.co.uk*

Although, I am a fervent believer in buying direct from the vineyard or from independent merchants, a special mention in dispatches must go to Waitrose. As well as making their own English sparkling on the Leckford estate in Hampshire, this supermarket chain has been incredibly supportive of English wines, selling a wide range. About 60% of English wines sold through UK retail outlets is via Waitrose. Individual stores also feature local and regional wines, a policy that is a world away from some of the other major supermarkets' view of retail.

VINEYARD DOGS

Visiting wine estates frequently goes hand in paw with having adorable four-legged canines as the welcome committee. Below is a small homage to just a few of our favourite friends!

LANGHAM ESTATE

ROLAND

BUSTER

DAISY
EXTON PARK

ARTY
ST MARTINS

OAK
SANDRIDGE BARTON

ROSIE

LEO

SIMPSONS

WILLOUGHBY

WISTON

COATES & SEELY

TRUFFLE

TWIGLET

HUGO

HATTINGLEY VALLEY

REX

BEAR

ALFIE

HARROW & HOPE

BERTIE

BEKA

BOSUN

AMBRIEL

HAMBLEDON

Directory of Food Producers

There are so many wonderful small food producers in England and the ones below have been chosen for their proximity to the wine estates, with whom they are listed.

Acquerello – *acquerello.it*

Alsop & Walker – *alsopandwalker.co.uk*

Beals Farm – *bealsfarmcharcuterie.com*

Book & Bucket Cheese –
  thebookandbucketcheesecompany.co.uk

Bookham Harrison – *bookhamharrison.co.uk*

Chalk Stream Trout – *chalkstreamfoods.co.uk*

Charlies Trout – *charliestrout.co.uk*

Chesil Smokery – *chesilsmokery.co.uk*

Cornish Charcuterie – *cornishcharcuterie.co.uk*

Cornish Gouda – *cornishgouda.co.uk*

Cream Roll – *creamroll.uk*

Dorset Sea Salt – *dorsetseasalt.co.uk*

Ellies Dairy – *elliesdairy.blogspot.com*

Flint Owl Bakery – *flintowlbakery.com*

Gimblett Cheese – *gimblettcheese.co.uk*

Hampshire Cheese Company –
  hampshirecheesecompany.co.uk

Hodmedods – *hodmedods.co.uk*

High Weald Dairy – *highwealddairy.co.uk*

Jakes Artisan Foods – *jakesartisanfoods.co.uk*

Kingcott Dairy – *kingcottdairy.co.uk*

Lyburn Farm – *lyburnfarm.co.uk*

Moons Green – *moonsgreen.co.uk*

Nettlebed Creamery – *nettlebedcreamery.com*

Norbury Blue – *norburyblue.co.uk*

Parsonage Farm Charcuterie –
  parsonagefarmcharcuterie.com

Pesky Fish – *peskyfish.co.uk*

Pipers Farm – *pipersfarm.com*

Red Fox Fine Foods – *redfoxfinefoods.co.uk*

River Teign Shellfish – *riverteignshellfish.co.uk*

SC Salt – *sc-salt.co.uk*

Seafood & Eat It – *seafoodandeatit.co.uk*

Spring Smokery – *springssmokedsalmon.co.uk*

Sussex Gourmand – *sussexgourmand.com*

Tempus Foods – *tempusfoods.com*

The Tomato Stall – *thetomatostall.co.uk*

The Traditional Cheese Company –
  thetraditionalcheesedairy.co.uk

Verjuice – *verjuice.co.uk*

Village Made Cheese – *villagemaidcheese.co.uk*

Winchester Distillery – *winchesterdistillery.co.uk*

Winterdale Cheese – *winterdale.co.uk*

Weald Smokery – *wealdsmokery.co.uk*

W. Harvey and Company – *crabmeat.co.uk*

Index of Wine Producers

Index of Recipes

Index of Recipes by Wine Type

GLOSSARY OF WINE TERMS

ABV – percentage of alcohol by volume.

Assemblage – in wine terms, this is the skilful blending of multiple base wines to create a more complex final wine. It does not have to be blending of different grape varieties but can simply be wines of the same variety from different vineyards – the permutations are endless. In food terms, it's simply my word for using a variety of pre-prepared foods, such as cheeses, charcuterie or goods from the deli counter, to create a no-cook, no-stress cornucopia of delights such as an antipasti platter.

Blanc de Blancs – sparkling wines made purely from white grapes. Traditionally in the Champagne region and for most English wine producers these wines are 100% Chardonnay grapes. However, there are other white varieties permitted in Champagne, such as Arbane, and other sparkling regions occasionally use the term for sparkling wines made from other local white grapes.

Blanc de Noirs – sparkling wine made purely from red/black grapes but where the resultant wine is white rather than red or rosé in colour. Classically this would be either 100% Pinot Noir or a blend with Meunier.

Bottle fermentation – part of the classic method of making sparkling wine as used in the Champagne region and for most English sparkling wines. After the first fermentation with yeast, the secondary fermentation takes place in the bottle, which creates the all-essential bubbles!

Brut – a sparkling wine is defined in style according to the sugar added at dosage. Brut is most often seen on sparkling wines and officially must be less than 12g sugar per litre. Extra Brut has between 0g and 6g sugar and Brut Nature between 0g and 2g. Demi Secs have between 32g and 50g per litre, but do try them as they are charming; don't think of the sugar just as sweetness, but instead as giving rich, full yet balanced wine. *See also* Zero Dosage.

Classic or Traditional method – the classic method of making sparkling wines, using a secondary fermentation in bottle.

Crémant – a style of sparkling wine usually made with the traditional secondary fermentation in bottle. Often seen from other French wine regions outside of Champagne, such as Crémant de Loire, de Bordeaux, d'Alsace, often using other grape varieties than the Champenoise Holy Trinity of grapes, which are local to that region. Crémant is a style that is likely to increase in popularity, with its gentler fizz and good value price tag.

Cuvée – originally from the French word for tank or vat, this has come to be the term used for a final blend of sparkling or sometimes still wine.

Dosage – the small amount of sugar added to sparkling wine that has been made by the traditional method, after disgorging, before the final cork is applied to the bottle. Dosage is hugely important in allowing the winemaker to determine the end style of the wine. The measurement of sugar in grams per litre applies only to the amount added by dosage (usually a blend of wine and sugar, known as a *liqueur d'expedition*).

Field-blend – wines made from a single vineyard, which is planted with a myriad of different grape varieties grown, harvested and vinified in the cellar all together, rather than keeping the different varieties separate until the final blend.

IWSC – International Wine and Spirit Competition.

Lees – the dead yeast cells that remain after fermentation. Whilst it might not sound terribly appealing, wine left 'on the lees' has greater complexity. Traditional sparkling wines are aged for a considerable amount of time on the lees, allowing the autolytic process – the destruction of the cells by their own enzymes – to occur, ultimately giving the classic autolytic aromas of brioche or toast in sparkling wines.

Meunier – You will see this grape variety referred to as either Pinot Meunier or Meunier, which actually means miller in French, thanks to the flour like surface of the leaves!

Mouthfeel – also referred to as the 'texture' of a wine. It is the physical sensation you feel in your mouth when tasting, such as oiliness or creaminess.

Pét Nat – short for *Pétillant Naturel*, it is a natural sparkling wine made with minimal intervention. Also known as 'hipster bubbles'.

Terroir – a French word that could take years to explain fully, but fundamentally it is generally accepted to be the effect of the climate, soil and land – intrinsically every aspect of the vine's environment – on the taste of a wine.

Vintage and Non-Vintage (NV) – terms found on a wine label. Vintage denotes that the wine (or at least 85% of it!) comes from one harvest of one year. Non-Vintage is (or could be) a blend across different years, as happens with many sparkling wines when reserve wines from different years are blended to maintain a house style each year. Increasingly in the UK the term Multi-Vintage is being used in place of NV to combat the odd negative perception that NV are somehow less important than Vintage wines.

Vitis vinifera – most commercial vineyards across the world are planted with the grapevine of the species *vitis vinifera*. However, after the phylloxera plague of the late nineteenth century when an invasion of aphids chomped their way through most vineyards' roots across Europe, vineyards replanted *vitis vinifera* but grafted onto American rootstocks resistant to phylloxera.

Zero Dosage – quite a fashionable style of sparkling wine with no sugar added at dosage stage (although technically it can have up to 3g residual sugar per litre), giving it a racy acidity.

WALL OF PATRONS

Mark & Graham
Coates

Eric & Sue
Collington

Lionel & Caron
Fanshawe

Joy & Dave
Goodyear

Colette Grant
& Stuart Adams

Sarah Hicks &
Lucy Spooner
(No Fuss Catering)

Alice
Hohler

Kate
King

Leonie
Loudon

Earl & Countess
of Macclesfield

Malcolm
Mace

James & Amanda
Nott

Oxford
Angel

Alan & Joan
Revie

Lynne & Chris
Rodgers

Jim & Jo
Ryan

Lady
Dawn Shields

Murray Strachan
& Carol Ross

Sue
Sutcliffe

Danni
Tucker

Lynn Biggs &
Michael Stone

Mike & Jayne
Bradly Russell

Michael
Brodrick

Dianne & Mike
Dean

Ian
Dunn

David
Erskine-Hill

Jenny & Tony
Grevatt

Caroline & Steve
Halliday

Simon
Hawkins

Eva
Krispinussen

Peter & Jane
Leaver

Neil & Fiona
Lock

Sarah
Matini

Jonathan & Fiona
Muirhead

Jayne & Paul
Murphy

Ann-Marie
Rivers

Arthur & Janet
Robins

Tony & Sian
Robinson

Peter & Maureen
Smith

Katrina Smith &
Nick Cran-Crombie

Andrew & Janet
Stracey

David & Sorrel
Wade

Mike & Mary
Wilson-Jones

Jana
Yell

THANKS

Thank you! Grazie! Merci! Danke! Gracias! Obrigada!

When I first started writing this book, starting with a random thought that drifted into my head whilst I was half-watching a food programme on the sofa with a glass of wine in hand, and which gradually took shape and showed itself to be a project that had to be taken to fruition – I confess that I had no idea how hard it would be to limit myself to just thirty-three wine estates.

Like all projects in life, I could never have done this alone.

On the previous pages, you'll have seen my 'Wall of Thank Yous' to all the incredible people who have so generously helped this book come to publication. The original idea was simply to get this published, but a pandemic hit the world, there were no wine tours for almost two complete years and so Plan B was called for. Crowdfunding might seem like a modern phenomenon, but since Shakespeare's day, generous patrons have supported books, plays and the art world – and so I decided to privately approach people already known to me, who I knew already had an interest in the subject of food and wine. Without their help, this book would not have seen the blessing of an ISBN, let alone graced anyone's bookshelf! One of the rewards for becoming a patron was a bundle of Pinot Noir vines, so I'm hoping that in five years or so there will be a raft of micro vineyards across the UK in people's gardens!

The team at whitefox, especially Chris Wold and Caroline McArthur have been awe-inspiring in their patience, taking me from the initial conversation on a rainy day, being there with support every step of the way, including the odd bump in the road when I faltered – keeping me focused – I can never thank you enough (though a lifetime supply of G&T's whenever you are in Hampshire is a given of course!)

I found illustrator Chloe Robertson by chance and what a fortuitous search courtesy of Monsieur Google that was! I was looking for someone local to the vineyards in the South of England, someone whose style would elevate this project from a mere jumble of words to a truly beautiful book. Cue initial meeting in a local pub (that dates from 1714!) to chat through ideas – and I instantly felt that Chloe understood completely the feel and style I was looking for. Her calm creativity is truly fabulous – and I am very lucky to have had her as part of the team.

To all the Wine Estates featured, thank you for giving your permission to be included. Certainly, when I was setting up the book there were a few initial enquiries – 'How much will it cost us to be included?' – which truly quite shocked me. My immediate reply of 'nothing' obviously reassured them that they were on the list through the merits of their wine alone. Their support in reading through copy, and long-term support in helping to promote the book through their cellar doors and online to their loyal customers is beyond thanks. I am so incredibly grateful for their inclusion in this book – and of course for making such great wine in the first place!

P.S. – to all those who were not included due to space limitations, a heartfelt apology. This is just a tiny number of English Wine Estates whose wines I truly enjoy. And to Welsh wine-producing friends, with all the awards they have been winning recently – that's another book in itself!

To all the owners and teams at other wine estates around the world: I calculated that I've made somewhere just over 3,500 estate visits – that's a lot of stainless steel and even more barrels I've seen. But each one of you has welcomed me with such genuine hospitality and warmth on many occasions – truly a case of #begrateful for having met you all. May the future smile on you and your families (and grapes!)

Vineyard Dogs – on many a visit to a winery, the canine welcoming committee has been the first impression for a wine lover. An essential part of the team, they truly deserve their place in this book, not only for their inherent welcoming nature, but also for keeping viticulturalists, winemakers and their teams calm during the more challenging and stressful moments of grape-growing and winemaking.

Food Producers – throughout this book I've mentioned a few great producers (see the directory on page 180 for their websites).

They totally deserve a thank you for making the world in which we live more delicious. But those mentions barely scratch the surface of the wealth of artisans creating amazing foods in the UK. Do explore what is on your own doorstep – there are so many great local food festivals that are great places to start, or look up your regional food association, such as my own local one, Hampshire Fare, which have good lists of local food heroes.

The Wine Trade – a sweepingly large virtual hug to all those in the wine trade around the world that have been so helpful over the last 25 years, so many times offering selfless advice or putting me in touch with the right person in the right region. I tried writing down the names of the people I thought deserved a special mention, but the list ran into gazillions – so rather than unfairly name some and others not, I propose a toast to all of us who have the luck to work in this fabulous trade – and thank all those I've met and whose laughter and support I've never forgotten.

Clients of Love Wine Food Ltd – one of the great things about working with food and wine, and specifically with tours, is that you meet such truly lovely people. A very special thank you goes to the various London Livery Companies that I have the privilege of taking on wine tours each year – each unique in their own style, but equally all united with a long history of dedication to charitable and admirable good works.

Although all the above have been key, either in the creation of this book or supporting me throughout my career, naturally it is my family and friends who over so many years have given me the self-belief and foundation to get me to this point!

To my mother, Fay, and to Robin – thank you for just being you, for always believing and for always being there for me.

To Neil, Tania, Benedict and Ella (and Monty, too) – once this has been published, I promise we'll get more time to see each other – a picnic at the cricket perhaps?

To my extended family, especially Danni and Ralph and the girls – it's just good knowing you guys are in my corner – thank you for ALL the laughter.

To my Italian family – you welcomed me with open arms and treated me as one of your own. A heartfelt thank you that will never be enough for all the fabulous memories created together in Moncalieri, Cuneo, Kitzbühel, Porto Cervo and Brittany. You all remain in my heart always, even when pandemics and general life commitments keep us apart.

To all my friends – where to start? After the last two years of the world being turned upside down by a pandemic, friendships are more important than ever. So, to those of you who I've truly missed – thank you for being there – even when that was only possible at the end of a phone, or with a quick text you sent for absolutely no other reason than to quickly brighten my day. I'm not sure that I deserve to have such great people in my life – and hope you know how important you all are to me. Roll on getting back to seeing much more of you all!

To JK – aka the Silver Fox. Thanks for your endless support over the last quarter of a century and for some rather long lunches putting the world to rights (and for N&P's patience when we finally roll home).

To the A&C Crew – you know who you are! Late night grappa's on the Cilento Coast, POA in a posh hat at a wedding, birthdays halfway up a vineyard in Chile, sharing an OCD attitude to the straightness of cutlery, endless laughter over so many bottles of wine – both then and now and hopefully again in the future. A huge hug.

Finally, to my beloved Paul. Thank you for putting up with my quirky ways, thank you for being there at the end of each day even when I'm travelling away from you, thank you for sharing so many great times together, often by the sea (but letting you free in the Rialto market to buy asparagus on your own might have been a mistake!). Thank you for sharing your heart (even though I know that I share it with the blonde, albeit she's a four-legged one!) Here's to many more rugby matches, kayaking, competing for control in the kitchen, and general japes and adventures together x

ABOUT THE AUTHOR

Cindy-Marie Harvey feels incredibly fortunate to work in the wine trade – specifically designing wine tours and leading wine-loving clients around the most beautiful wine regions of the world. She has spent over a quarter of a century visiting and tasting her way from Chile, Argentina and Uruguay to the dramatic South Island of New Zealand, from the châteaux of the Left Bank in Bordeaux to stunningly beautiful vineyards in northern Italy and beyond. Add to this heavenly blend the challenge of pairing the best wine and food matches for lunches at wine estates or showcasing regional wines over dinner at a Slow Food Osteria… it's like living in a permanent state of preparation for a supper party with friends – what better job could there be?

Although her first experience of English wine, more than four decades ago, was not something she was keen to quickly repeat, over the intervening years it has been a fascinating journey to mark the dedication and achievement of winemakers in her home country.

Since her favourite hobby is to surround herself with recipe books (some mainstream, some eclectic and in a variety of languages picked up on her travels), her overactive brain seems to be forever thinking about food and wine pairings across the flavour spectrum. Even when swimming, her thoughts regularly ponder what Christmas canapés might work with Nebbiolo or maybe Sancerre or Bacchus!

Although she considers herself incredibly honoured to have met and made great friends throughout the wine trade, Cindy-Marie has no commercial affiliation with any of the wine estates mentioned, nor have they paid for their inclusion in this book. Their wines have simply been chosen out of her total and utter belief in their deliciousness and food friendliness!